# THE SACRIFICE OF GOD

# THE SACRIFICE OF GOD

## *A Holistic Theory of Atonement*

### JOHN MOSES

Foreword by
### STEPHEN SYKES
*Bishop of Ely*

The Canterbury Press
Norwich

FOR
RACHEL
RICHARD
AND
CATHERINE

# Foreword

There can be no sensible participation in the Decade of Evangelism unless the church has a firm grasp upon the doctrine of the atonement. But it is precisely the association of evangelism with a frankly debased theology of threat, guilt and manipulation which makes the whole project so apparently uncertain.

John Moses has done the church a considerable favour by daring to sketch the outline of what he calls a 'holistic theory' of atonement. Holistic thinking is not a big TOE (Theory of Everything), but a new horizon or framework, characterised by patterns of interdependence, elements of necessity and chance, the motif of life and death and life, and the promise of coherence.

The book challenges the compartmentalized thinking which allows us to be scientific and modern with one part of our minds and ritualistic and medieval with another. It is a major strength of the presentation that sacrifice is made central to the theory. Thus both mainstream Christian doctrine and eucharistic spirituality are included within the horizons of the theory. And the necessary link between the once-for-all sacrifice of the cross and our own lives, Moses provides through the idea of the living symbol, drawing upon thoughts from Jung and Tillich among others.

Enough has been said, I trust, to show that this is a wide-ranging and highly instructive work of synthesis. Moses has helped his readers by writing in a clear, uncluttered and engaging style. I know there will be many who will be helped and inspired by it; and encouraged to whole-hearted participation in an evangelism which is inseparable from the life of the redeemed people of God.

*Easter Eve 1992*                    ✠ STEPHEN ELY

# Contents

# ACKNOWLEDGEMENTS

I have been greatly assisted by a large number of people during the writing of this book, and I am glad to acknowledge how much I owe:

to the Bishop of Chelmsford and to colleagues within the residentiary chapter and staff of Chelmsford Cathedral for encouragement and support during a period of sabbatical study leave;

to the President and Fellows of Wolfson College, Cambridge, for a Visiting Fellowship during the Lent and Easter Terms of 1987;

to the Right Reverend Stephen Sykes for critical comment and encouragement as I attempted to share my thinking at an early stage and for the Foreword to this book that he has now generously written;

to the Trustees of the Hockerill Educational Foundation and of the Bethune-Baker Fund of the University of Cambridge for financial assistance;

to the Mother Abbess and Sisters of the Benedictine Community of St Mary's Abbey at West Malling in Kent for their hospitality on so many occasions;

to Mrs Anita Butt, Miss Janet Firman and Mr Stanley Hill who have done so much in the typing and preparation of this manuscript for publication;

and to my wife, Susan, whose thinking has stimulated my thinking, and whose forbearance has made it possible to complete the writing.

I am glad to acknowledge also the permission that has been granted to quote directly from a large number of published works. Every attempt has been made to secure permission to use copyright material, and all such material is acknowledged either in the text or in the notes at the end of this book.

# Preface

The mystery of death and resurrection lies at the heart of the Christian gospel, but there are many to whom the great theories of atonement fail to speak persuasively. It was Luther's triumphant affirmation that the cross tests everything,[1] and yet it is necessary to ask if such a comprehensive claim can be sustained. The New Testament tells of God's purpose to reconcile *all things* through Christ, making peace by the blood of His cross.[2] Theories of atonement which lead to an exclusive preoccupation with personal salvation must be judged, therefore, to be inadequate. There are dimensions that are personal and social, corporate and cosmic. A contemporary interpretation of atonement theology must explore the relationship of the cross to the whole fabric of life.

Theories of atonement can never be divorced from our understanding of the world in which we live. Studies in atonement theology, while attempting to remain faithful to the insights of scripture and tradition, have always reflected the thought-forms of their age. There have been those who have looked forward to the time when there might be a radical restatement of atonement theology.[3] It would be presumptuous to suggest that this book provides such a restatement. I am too mindful of the magnitude of the task and of the limitations of what has been done. But it is the conviction of this book that a restatement of the mystery of atonement is required if we are to speak to a world which is increasingly characterised by a holistic approach to life, by an awareness of the essential at-one-ness of all things.

This book is an essay in Christian theology. Its starting-point is the world, and it proceeds from the conviction that we have within the Christian revelation all the raw material we need to make sense of our world. Christian theology will always be on its guard against any suggestion that the wisdom of God and the wisdom of the world are one and the same thing;[4] but *a holistic theory of atonement* attempts an exposition of the word of the cross which shows how the rationality and coherence of Christian faith correspond with the rationality and coherence of the world.

There is an urgent need to attempt from the standpoint of Christian faith a comprehensive and systematic interpretation of the world. It is entirely legitimate to ask if there is a world-view that Christian theology can put forward which can be regarded as authentic in our world. Is it possible to ascribe to the cross a place of absolute primacy within such a scheme of things? Is it possible to speak of 'a total, universal Christ, a Christ who is the All-in-Everything'?[5] It is the submission of this book that only a holistic theory can begin to meet these requirements.

But this preface is bound to acknowledge the inadequacies of what has been attempted. First, I am aware of the incompleteness of what has been written. Its terms of reference are wide-ranging, but it does little more than touch briefly upon large areas of theological enquiry. There are many places where it would be desirable to develop the argument at far greater length; but it has seemed right to bring within the compass of this book the search for wholeness, the task of theology, the meaning of sacrifice, the work of Christ, the theories of atonement, the mystery of atonement, and the Christian understanding of life in God. Secondly, I am mindful of the fact that the numerous references to *man* and to *mankind* will be greatly regretted by those who seek a wider use of inclusive language. These words are used in their generic sense. It is only the absence of simple and commonly accepted alternatives which has made it necessary to fall back on these traditional forms. Thirdly, I recognise the extent to which I have drawn upon the writings of other people. I have acknowledged my indebtedness to a large number of writers, but I know how easily the actual words that have been used by others can be reproduced unwittingly. I hope this has not happened.

What I have been feeling after will always escape our

understanding. Atonement is a mystery that we receive in faith. It is not easy to write about God and His revelation and His work of redemption in Jesus Christ in a world where the vocabulary and the basic concepts of Christian faith are scarcely recognised. Christian theology must, therefore, have an edge that is apologetic and evangelistic. Bonhoeffer's word remains: 'It is not for us to prophesy the day (though the day will come) when men will once more be called so to utter the word of God that the world will be changed and renewed by it'.[6] Our world has a profound sense of the interdependence of all things. Could it be that our understanding of the world requires a new exposition of atonement theology? Could it be that our understanding of atonement theology provides a pattern of interpretation for the contemporary world?

*Chelmsford*                                    JOHN MOSES

# PART I

# THE SEARCH FOR WHOLENESS

*Chapter 1*

# The Search for Wholeness

Christian hope is confidence in the power of God. Its distinguishing characteristic is the conviction that God's purposes are to be found in Jesus Christ. These purposes, which are discerned within the mysteries of faith, speak of a plan for the fullness of time: that all things – things in heaven and things on earth – shall be united in Christ.[1]

The extraordinary claim that God will be all in all[2] lies at the heart of the Christian doctrine of atonement. It is here that Christian hope finds its fullest expression. There is in atonement theology the belief that beyond the contradictions of our world there lies some overwhelming experience of unity. It is the judgement of Christian faith that in Jesus 'the fullness of God was pleased to dwell, and through Him to reconcile all things, whether on earth or in heaven, making peace by the blood of His cross'.[3]

There is a direct relationship, therefore, between the cross and all that is meant by atonement. The cross is the element of uncompromising and inescapable sacrifice at the centre of Christian faith. To speak of the mystery of atonement is to wrestle with the meaning of the cross. It was Luther's triumphant affirmation that the cross tests everything.[4] But is it possible to argue that the cross, which continues to defy all rational explanation, provides some vital connection, drawing together and unifying in some comprehensive structure all that Christian theology has to say?

The Christian understanding of atonement requires us to look at the Christian revelation in its entirety. All that must be said about God and the created order, about man, about the reality of evil, about the work of Christ, about the

3

experience of redemption, about the end of all things provide
the backcloth for an exposition of the cross. And the possibilities that are contained within the Christian hope lead inevitably to questions concerning God's purposes. Where does it
all lead? Is there some vision that transcends our experience
of dissolution and decay? What is our final atonement?

The church does not think through its faith in isolation
from the world. It is in the world that we find God. It is in
the centre of life that we find the meaning of faith. Christian
doctrine evolves through a long process of continuing dialogue. Atonement theology is no exception. No theory of
atonement can claim exclusive biblical authority. The church
has never provided a definitive statement of the meaning of
the cross. It could not have done so. The cross is too significant within the experience of the church to be constrained
within the language, the imagery, of any one age. The great
theories of atonement, while remaining faithful to the insights
of scripture, have invariably reflected the structures, the
thought-forms, the vocabulary, the aspirations of their
respective ages.

It is always part of the work of Christian apologetic to
explore the connections between the rationality and coherence of Christian faith and the rationality and coherence of the
world as we perceive it. If religion has been disowned and
disregarded by recent generations, and especially in the
western world, it is at least in part because it is no longer
seen to relate to people's experience of life and to illuminate
it. There is an urgent need to attempt, from the standpoint
of Christian faith, a comprehensive and systematic understanding of the world. There is no consensus within society
to which Christian theology can appeal. It is only possible to
proceed in the light of the ancient principle of faith seeking
understanding. But if it is possible to interpret our world
aright, wrestling with the Christian tradition in the light of
contemporary knowledge, then it might be possible to recover
for Christian theology its ancient claim to be the discipline
of coherence because it speaks of the God who holds within
Himself the whole of being.

The idea of atonement is notoriously complex, but the

English rendering of the word as at-one-ment captures the inner meaning and relates directly to the predominant pattern that is encountered on every side. It is one of the paradoxes of our tormented world that, in spite of a universal experience of estrangement, there is to be found a growing recognition of the interdependence of all things. There has always been some intuitive awareness of the depths of meaning and belonging which have found expression in the ancient myths, in the writings of the poets, in the knowledge of the mystics, in the commonplace experiences which provide moments of insight. Fundamental questions concerning the purposes of life continue to present themselves, but empirical knowledge requires a new conceptual framework in which we can set the search for wholeness.

This search for wholeness is not invalidated by the ambiguities of life. The theme of alienation has been used by theologians and philosophers, political theorists and social scientists, psychologists and psychiatrists, writers, dramatists and musicians to interpret the experience of fragmentation, confusion and conflict. Doris Lessing tells in *The Golden Note-Book* the story of a woman caught up in the turmoil of her personal relationships and of the political struggles of her generation. She reflects that life is 'crude, unfinished, raw, tentative'; but she insists that 'the raw unfinished quality in my life was precisely what was valuable in it'.[5]

It is a necessary part of the pain of the journey to allow the contradictions of our experience to bear in upon us. They must not be denied. But alienation has wider connotations. The accumulated torments of the world are too grievous and too destructive to be accommodated merely as the growing pains of our personal maturity. Alienation has been expressed as man looking upon himself with the eyes of a stranger.[6] Our age has no monopoly of tragedy, but part of the intolerable truth of our time is lived out in deeply damaged and disordered personalities, in the gross injustices of an international world-order, in the ancient bigotries of race and religion, in the death-wish that seems to possess the race.

It is no part of our task to seek some facile pattern of unity that can be imposed upon the warring elements. It is to affirm, however, that there is in so many areas of knowledge and experience some recognition of the essential unity of life. The silent conviction that 'originally or ideally or potentially a pattern of integration does exist'[7] is too strong and too powerfully supported by all the evidence to be dismissed as a convenient device for managing with some degree of confidence and toleration the bitter-sweet experience of life. The search for wholeness encompasses the contradictions and the complexities. It is inseparable from all the facts that confront us. It is a fundamental part of the rationality and coherence of our world. Could it be that our understanding of the contemporary world requires a new exposition of atonement theology? Could it be that our understanding of atonement theology provides a pattern of interpretation for the contemporary world?

# Chapter 2

# The Living World

Christian theology is required to take account of all that happens in the world. Its perception of the truth is informed by scripture, tradition and reason; but these continuously interacting resources have one notable characteristic – namely, the conviction that God acts in the world, in history, in the lives of nations and of individuals. It might provide its own rigorous and prophetic interpretation but it cannot ignore the processes of life within which, according to the insights of the Christian revelation, God chooses to work.

It is, therefore, appropriate for the student of Christian atonement theology to turn in the first instance to those areas of knowledge and experience where there is some recognition of the holistic character of the world and to enquire concerning the patterns that might be discerned. Insights must be checked and counter-checked. It cannot be assumed that the patterns of the world will necessarily correspond with the purposes of God as Christian theology has traditionally expounded them. But the possibility that these patterns might provide the framework for a comprehensive exposition of the Christian revelation, signs of the unity which has its origin and its fulfilment in God, is too compelling to be lightly abandoned.

First, there is an awareness of the universe as an open, dynamic, interdependent and indivisible whole. Modern physics has brought about great changes in our understanding of space and time, of matter, of the elementary particles, of cause and effect. It is no longer possible to think of the universe as a closed system, fixed, static, self-contained. The Newtonian model presupposed a world of solid bodies moving in time and space. Relativity theories and quantum theory have brought us beyond such a world-picture. Space and time cannot be separated. There is a space-time continuum in which the cosmic processes unfold; and there is an openness to the future in these processes that had not previously been envisaged. Atomic and sub-atomic physics have explored the dynamic nature of matter. The atoms which were believed to constitute the world of matter are now known to be complex and composite systems. These sub-atomic units appear as particles and waves. Matter is full of activity. It is a living world which maintains its stability through complex patterns of organisation and relationship. The properties of particles are made known through their interaction with their environment. Indeed, matter should properly be regarded, together with time and space, as aspects of one interdependent entity.

One attempt to provide a single evolutionary science which can describe the story of our planet has been made by James Lovelock who, building upon the classical Darwinian theory of evolution by natural selection, has argued that the evolution of all species of organisms and the evolution of their material environment are so inseparably bound up with each other that they constitute a single system.[1] His adoption of Gaia, the Greek goddess of the earth, as the embodiment of his hypothesis is concerned to provide a way of looking at the earth as a single and self-regulating organism, a coherent life system.

It is implicit in this approach to a new and unified vision of the earth and of the life sciences that creation is incomplete. There are elements in the process that can only be described by words like necessity and chance, spontaneity and choice. There appears to be great waste, and yet the processes of evolution achieve coherence through the adaptation of organisms to their environment. Physicists, chemists and biologists have shown that the evolution of life displays both a remarkable spontaneity and an ordered interaction. The living world appears to possess endless possibilities. Matter has the power to form more varied and sophisticated complexes. Evolution is the means whereby the potentialities that are present in life are managed and developed. Evolution takes place as simple molecules come together to form complexes that are able to reproduce themselves; and yet this process can only be maintained through the interaction of these molecules with their environment. Organisms learn to adapt or they perish; and natural selection is the means whereby adaptations, mutations, movements forward in the process of evolution are actually realised.

Nature has a remarkable capacity to organise itself as forms of life progress through the integration of electrons and protons, the association of atoms in living molecules, the co-ordination of cells in complex organisms. The cell is a system of immense complexity and activity. All plants and animals are made up of cells, and these are characterised both by a differentiation of function and by co-operative activity. It is by exercising their different functions that the cells constitute the organisms of which they are parts. There is autonomy and co-ordination.

The relationship between the parts and the whole and their interaction upon each other is fundamental to the whole process. Indeed, the way in which the parts and the whole interact gives a fascinating insight into the development of the entire process. And yet the pattern of the activity by which the system is known is something that is communicated by the whole to its parts. The human brain can be cited as an example of how these things work. The brain is a system. It consists of a thousand million million macromolecules. It is constantly receiving information and sending out messages; but its operation is not determined by the innumerable macromolecules. It is the brain, the organism taken as a whole with its reservoir of memories, its established patterns of behaviour, its continuing identity, which gives order and direction to the constantly changing and reconstituted parts. The brain is an important system co-ordinating and controlling subordinate systems. The brain, the body, the species are all systems of varying degrees of sophistication and superiority.[2] Beyond the cells and the organisms of which they form essential parts lies the hierarchy of systems which man explores and of which man himself forms a part.

Secondly, man's relationship both with the universe at large and with the planet that he inhabits demonstrates the extent to which the human species forms part of the whole process of continuing creation. The biblical myths affirm that man is made in the image of God. They do not deny that he is formed of the dust of the ground. Man belongs to nature and cannot sustain his life without the ecological balance that has been achieved. The atmosphere, the oceans, the rain forests, all play their part in securing the conditions that make for life and for the continuation of life.

Man has evolved to the point where he is able to understand, to articulate and to participate consciously in the processes of life; but he remains – together with animals, plants and bacteria – a part of one living world. Some of man's capacities are present in rudimentary forms in the animal creation – the ability to form relationships for the purposes of survival, reproduction, kinship or the performance of a common task; the capacity to communicate; the ability to learn from experience and to communicate that learning. Man differs in significant respects, however, in his self-awareness; in his capacity for abstract thought; in his appreciation of natural beauty; in his perception of moral and spiritual values and realities; in his ability to transcend his immediate environment, seeking his identity and meaning in someone or something that lies beyond himself; and in his power to determine to a unique degree his own continuing evolution or his self-destruction.

It is this last consideration that is of greatest moment. Man is involved in the life of the universe to a far greater degree than has ever before been envisaged. He is a product of the evolving continuity of the universe, and he is caught up in the process with ever-increasing insight and responsibility. In his relation to the environment, man now possesses the power to disturb the balance of nature to the disadvantage of his own species and of all other forms of life. There is a relationship of continuous interaction for better or for worse between man and the natural environment.

It is impossible to avoid this awareness of the unity of all living things. The human species forms 'one closely interlocked network of ecological relationships' with all other living organisms.[3] Bacteria, fungi, plants, animals and the human species constitute one flesh.[4] There is a wholeness, an at-one-ness, about the world around and within us. 'It is easy to elevate these facts into a pretentious scheme of the whole living world as one "organism". Yet there is a sense in which this is true. It is difficult to exaggerate our interdependence.'[5]

Thirdly, man is a social animal. He is bound to his species, to society and to history in a seemingly endless variety of ways. All that we know about the identity and personality of the individual, about the relationships and institutions that constitute society, about patterns of behaviour, about the formation of ethical and social values, about our common history, suggest that men and women are all bound up in one another. We belong together.

The pattern of the life of an individual is shaped by factors that are physical and psychological, historical and cultural, social and personal. Heredity is a powerful determining force, but nature and nurture combine to shape the raw material and this is constantly exposed to the great range of influences that bear upon it. An individual must be seen in his entirety. There is an area of freedom. Choices are made; and, although these choices are determined by personal and social consider-ations of which there may be no great awareness, there is a sense in which people become what they choose to be. Family characteristics repeat themselves, but personality is not fixed and immutable. It evolves in the light of the whole of our experience.

Society has been likened to a stage populated by living actors.[6] Patterns of behaviour are shaped by a complex web of assumptions and expectations, and yet this web can be broken by expressions of individuality and it will adapt and change and elicit different responses as society moves on. It is in the continuing interaction of society upon individuals and of individuals upon society that changes take place. We are shaped by society and society is shaped by us. Individuals demand the acceptance and recognition of society. Society requires our recognition and participation. The interaction is both determined and desired. Established social norms require consent. Behaviour is socially conditioned. Personal attitudes and values, including prejudices and fears, are acquired and learnt. The sense of right and wrong is shaped by the influence of the family, the school, the peer group, the media; and these in turn are informed by the accumulated wisdom and experience of society which are constantly being adapted by new insights and demands. This is not to suggest that all values are relative, culturally conditioned. There are variations in the moral codes that societies adopt; different circumstances demand that the primary valuations are worked out in different ways; and yet there is evidence of a common humanity which betrays its innate sense of universal morality in expressions of moral outrage which cut across cultural and ideological boundaries. There is an increasingly informed awareness of the corporate nature of the life of the human species.

The idea of corporate personality has depths of meaning that have not been fully explored. The life-stories of individuals are instructive. Legal concepts, the framework of law and order, the administration of justice assume a high degree of personal responsibility. This cannot be removed; but some qualification is required in the light of our understanding of personal and corporate guilt in patterns of deviation and criminality. A causal connection was made in earlier generations between poverty and crime; but there is now a recognition of the environmental factors, the emotional deprivations, and the whole *mores* of a society which create the vulnerability, and at times even the culpability, of the offender, the victim and the society of which they are both members.

The life-stories of nations are no less instructive. Leo Tolstoy's great novel *War and Peace* portrays Russian life at the time of the ill-fated Napoleonic Expedition of 1812, but his picture is shot through with his awareness of our corporate responsibility. He defines history as 'the unconscious, universal, swarm-life of mankind'.[7] It is not sufficient to consider the actions and motivations of kings and politicians and generals. Tolstoy is mindful of the need to look beneath the surface of an historical event and enquire into the activity of the whole people. 'Every man lives for himself, using his freedom to attain his personal aims, and feels with his whole being that he can at any moment perform or not perform this or that action; but, so soon as he has done it, that action accomplished at a certain moment in time becomes irrevocable and belongs to history'.[8] And so it is that Tolstoy locates in the particular – or, to be more precise, in the multiplicity of particulars – the general burden of responsibility for the story of the race.

Fourthly, the mutual needs and interests of nations – political and economic – are demanding new structures which recognise the interdependence of all people. Political ideology, race, colour, religion continue to command passionate allegiances and to inflict deep wounds. Nations – like individuals – act in the light of their own perceived self-interest. But the age-old search for a more responsible management of human society has taken on in recent generations an international dimension. The League of Nations and the United Nations Organisation were both brought into being in the hope that they might provide a forum for consultation and for international negotiation and agreement. Regional groupings have been established for the purposes of defence, trade and communication; and these groupings invariably carry some consequence for the political sovereignty of independent nation states. The rapidly changing patterns of economic and social life have brought an ever-increasing awareness of our interdependence. They are requiring us to rediscover the ancient insight that ethics and law, politics and economics, cannot be disentangled from each other within the corporate life of the body politic.

Few studies have done more in recent years to address the challenge that mankind is now becoming a single community than the report of the *International Commission on International Development Issues* in 1980. The Commission addressed the familiar problems: the massive and continuing growth of the world's population; the absolute poverty in which vast numbers of people are condemned to live; world development, the monetary system, industrialisation, technology and trade; peace and disarmament; the ecological balance and especially the protection of the environment, the use of energy, the management of the resources of the ocean; and the wider political questions of international negotiation and organization.

The thrust of the Commission's report was to draw attention to the extent to which the world is now a fragile and interlocking system, whether for its people, its ecology, or its resources.[9] The report tried to help people see how their daily lives and jobs are bound up with those of other people all over the world.[10] Self-interest alone demands that nations and regional groupings shall no longer act as isolated and independent units. The desired goals are peace and plenty and justice but these will require sacrifices, and the sacrifices will be greater for those with the power and the resources to bear them.[11] The political and economic complexities of life are such that the nations of the world – like the particles of matter within the atom, or the cells within the organism, or the human species in relation to its environment, or individuals within society – constitute 'a system of many different components interacting with one another – changes in one affecting all the rest'.[12] It is all one world and we are members one of another.

Fifthly, the pleas for a holistic approach to medicine are consistent with the search for wholeness that can be discerned in so many other spheres. The abandonment of mechanical models in attempting to explain the nature of the universe, the structure of matter and the evolution of life has been matched by a recognition of the inadequacy of comparable models in the approach to health and healing. Physical and mental health, emotional and spiritual vitality, personal and social relations are the varied components that interact within the life of an individual. Holistic medicine recognises the interplay of all these things.

This awareness of the wholeness of the person belongs to an ancient tradition which, rediscovered in a variety of modern forms, does not call in question the massive advances in man's medical knowledge and treatment of diseases through the adoption of the bio-medical model. Ancient traditions of folk medicine were concerned to address themselves to the whole man; and the deployment of religion and magic in the medical practices of primitive man spoke of wider dimensions in the understanding of disorder and disease. In ancient India, health was believed to require a balance of the elementary substances of the body. In ancient China, health was thought to depend on the balance of the Yin and the Yang, the masculine and feminine principles, representing activity and passivity, light and darkness, the heavens and the earth. In ancient Greece, the harmony of the four humours was judged to be necessary for the maintenance of health; and the concept of humours, which dominated European thought throughout the medieval period, assumed a psychosomatic approach to healing which looked for the interplay of these vital elements.

The view of Descartes, the seventeenth century French philosopher, that the human body is a machine had important consequences for medical thought and practice. No plea for a holistic approach to health can diminish the achievements of the last two centuries; and the transformation that has been seen in the world of medicine has been assisted by developments in public health, through improvements in hygiene and sanitation, the provision of better housing, better nutrition, a higher standard of living. These things have meant that in the developed countries there has been throughout this century a remarkable increase in people's life expectancy. And yet there is concern that certain basic assumptions remain unchallenged at a practical working level. The social, psychological and behavioural dimensions of illness cannot be accommodated within the framework provided by the biomedical model. Meanwhile, developments in our understanding of the human mind and personality, the practice of psychiatry, combined with new insights in physiology, demand a recognition of the interaction of mind and body. Psychosomatic theory and practice, psychosomatic medicine, prepared the way for holistic medicine.

Holistic medicine has come to mean many things. Its main thrust, however, is the concern to see the person in his entirety and to respond to him as a complete person. The various ingredients of a person's experience – physical, psychological and social – are all interconnected. Health is not the absence of disease. Disease is not merely the disturbance or dislocation of health. Illness can be precipitated by profound anxiety, suppressed anger and resentment, unresolved conflict, guilt, the refusal or inability to love ourselves, to accept and to own what we are. Health and disease are not to be seen only in relation to each other, but in relation to the human organism in its entirety. The question to be asked is not merely, 'What is the cause of this illness?'; but 'Why does *this* person have *this* disease *now*?'[13]

Two contemporary developments – therapeutic centres for the treatment of cancer patients and hospices for the care of the dying – approach their work on the basis of the principles that lie at the heart of holistic medicine: that a person is a unique individual; that a person must be considered in relation to all aspects of his life; that a person must be involved – actively and knowledgeably – in his own treatment; that a person must be encouraged to bring into play his own self-healing and self-repair systems.[14]

Some who have experience of the treatment of cancer patients have asked questions about the connection between the personality and the emotional health of the patient and the progress of the disease. It has long since been recognised that emotional disorders can cause some medical problems, but the idea that there might be a psychosomatic basis for cancer has been resisted.[15] It is a commonplace to hear people speak of someone fighting to live or losing the will to live. Medical research suggests that despair, panic, fear, exasperation can inhibit the full engagement of the healing resources of the human brain, whereas a strong determination to live and great expectations can facilitate the ability of the brain to generate chemical changes in the body.[16] Several studies suggest that the appearance of cancer within the body involves both biological and psychological processes; that the crucial factor can be a crisis which threatens something right at the heart of the person's identity, and that mental, emotional and spiritual health can play a vital part in the treatment of the patient. And yet the questions remain. Why do some succeed and others fail? How do we account for the anomalies that life presents? Is it merely a matter of chance, or is there some additional factor which has its roots deep in the ground of a person's own being which makes connections for good or for ill with heredity and environment and physical and mental health and self-motivation?

The hospice recognises that, where there is opportunity to do so, preparation for dying is vital both for the person and for the family. The hospice provides an environment in which the dying can be cared for without pretence, retaining their dignity, sharing the fact of their approaching death as fully as possible with family and friends, recognising that death is part of life. Death is no longer seen as being in any sense a failure by patients, family or staff. There can be a restoration to wholeness for all who are involved which transcends the process of physical decay and death.

Sixthly, the creative arts tell of the fundamental human search for wholeness, albeit in ways that can be both illuminating and disturbing. Art refuses to be detached from life. It is born of the artist's engagement with himself and with all around him. It is a human activity and yet it is never entirely a form of individual self-expression. Dostoyevsky's aim as a writer was 'to find the man in man'.[17] Gauguin's concern as a painter was to get beyond the sensations of the eye and 'evoke the inner life of man in the mysterious centre of the mind'.[18]

Art is the means whereby the artist conveys to others all that he experiences, and in that act he joins others together with himself. The only thing that matters is its integrity. Is it true? Or is it an exercise in deception, a portrayal of the mask rather than an expression of what is actually there? The artist uses his medium to make unexpected connections – impressions, situations, personalities, relationships, experiences, passions, ideas. He brings his creative curiosity, his interpretative skill, to bear upon his subject. He holds up a mirror to the face of his own world. His work makes visible the things that are hidden. It is when the artist is able to take us beyond the contemporary scene and set our immediate concerns within the context of the universal human drama that his work takes on an additional quality of transcendence, of greatness.

It is not sufficient to portray the truth. It is necessary to participate fully in the work. The authority of the artist and the integrity of the work will be determined by the extent to which these two requirements can be met. Wilfred Owen, perhaps the most notable English poet of the First World War, wrote, 'My subject is War and the pity of War. The Poetry is in the pity'.[19] He might have added that the pity was born of his own pain. There is a special kind of sensitivity which enables the artist to explore and to expose. There is contact. There is compulsion. There is understanding. There is pain. The artist's work may well disturb. Indeed, if it fails to disturb, it may mean that it has failed to penetrate the bland certainties with which we console ourselves. But beyond the emptiness and the torment, the sense that the artist can only express a small part of what he sees and feels, there lies some new perception of the truth, the vitality, the humour, the pathos of our condition.

It is the engagement of the artist with the whole of his experience that makes it possible to understand something of the torment that afflicts so many creative artists. Less imprisoned by the constraints of convention, they keep in touch with the raw material of their own inner lives and of ours. There is a relation between society and its creative minds. The pain of the world will inform our writers, painters, musicians, sculptors. And yet the desire to be in touch with the deepest rhythms of life persists, and art in its many forms retains its ancient power to connect with the fundamental forces of the world and give some sense of identity and purpose. There is still within people 'a blind grasping out for their own wholeness',[20] and the artist can provide the confidence to enter the darkness of an unfamiliar world.

Peter Shaffer's portrayal of Mozart depicts the young musician, provocative and irrepressible, taunting the court officials with his irreverence but expressing this sense of the wholeness of things that can be captured in an opera as the composer draws together the thoughts and the feelings and the themes and interweaves them in one great crescendo. 'I tell you I want to write a finale lasting half an hour! A quartet becoming a quintet becoming a sextet. On and on, wider and wider – all the sounds multiplying and rising together – and then together making a sound entirely new'.[21] But Mozart goes on to give his understanding of the importance of this achievement: 'I bet you that's how God hears the world. Millions of sounds at once and mixing in His ear to become an unending music, unimaginable to us! That's our job we composers: to combine the inner minds of him and him and her and her – the thoughts of chambermaids and Court Composers – and then turn the audience into God.'[22]

And yet within this passionate exposition of the task of the composer, there is to be found an acknowledgement of the special place of every word and every note. Herbert Butterfield uses the analogy of a Beethoven symphony to remind us that 'the point is not saved up until the end, the whole of it is not a mere preparation for a beauty that is only to be achieved in the last bar. And although in a sense the end may lie in the architecture of the whole, still in another sense each moment of it has its own self-justification, each note in its particular context as valuable as any other note'.[23] Each note has its place, each word, each stroke of the brush, each blow of the hammer and chisel. Each one relates to all that has gone before and to all that will come after. Each one retains its identity and integrity but, abandoning its independence, is taken up in a great movement forward, and thus makes its unique and necessary contribution to the whole.

*Chapter 3*

# A Holistic Theory

The living world displays patterns of association which speak of the essential unity of life, the inter-relatedness of all things. These patterns of association cannot be confused with the pattern of atonement which Christian theology locates in the death and resurrection of Jesus. The common theme of the Old and the New Testaments is God's covenant relationship with His people; but the context is one of creation and redemption, and the story is shot through with insights which demand that God's work of atonement has dimensions that are personal and social and cosmic. Definitions and theories of atonement must therefore be set within a broad frame.

But the distinguishing mark of Christian theology is the word of the cross. Those who attempt to discern in the patterns of association that have been identified signs of the Christian mystery of atonement will be mindful of Luther's uncompromising statement that no one can be called a theologian 'who looks upon the invisible things of God as though they were clearly perceptible in those things which have actually happened. He deserves to be called a theologian, however, who comprehends the visible and manifest things of God through suffering and the Cross'.[1]

The centrality of the cross requires a new appreciation of sacrifice in the light of the images that belong to the contemporary world; but any emphasis upon sacrifice – including the sacrifice of the cross – must be set within a broad frame and take full account of the interlocking patterns that confront the observer on every side.

It is over twenty years since an appeal was made for a general conceptual framework, transcending that of traditional science, because of the recognition that in many disciplines, and especially in the natural and human sciences, 'we are forced . . . to deal with complexities, wholes, systems, organisations'.[2] It is perfectly permissible for Christian theology to seek a new framework – consistent both with the insights of scripture and with the knowledge of our world – within which the mysteries of faith can be explored. This is not to abandon the wisdom of God, which is the word of the cross, for the wisdom of the world.[3] An acknowledgement of the holistic character of the world does not mean that the Christian revelation in its entirety or the Christian doctrine of atonement in particular can be contained within some abstract principle of science or philosophy.

The Christian hope that God will be all in all cannot be contained within any one theory. Successive conceptual frameworks have provided the context within which the Christian revelation has been examined and proclaimed. All theories of atonement give us ways of looking at the meaning of life. They provide insights which assist us as we wrestle with the meaning of the cross. The search for wholeness is a conspicuous feature of contemporary experience. The awareness of the essential at-one-ness of life is a distinguishing mark of our world. If the patterns of association that are to be found in so many areas have been traced correctly – albeit in brief outline – can it be that we shall find within these patterns the new conceptual framework within which we are required to work? Can it be that a new understanding of atonement theology – a holistic theory – is called for? And this term – a *holistic* theory of atonement – would not be inappropriate either by reason of all that is happening in the world or by reason of the meaning of the word which speaks of wholeness, completeness, at-one-ment. There is only one caveat that must be made even at this stage if the Christian tradition is to remain true to itself. The search for wholeness incorporates the element of sacrifice. A holistic theory of atonement requires a cross.

What are the things of which Christianity must take account as it attempts to speak of God's work of reconciliation in Christ? What are the patterns that appear to correspond as theology and science reflect upon the raw material of their respective disciplines? What are the common characteristics to be found in these areas of knowledge and experience? What are the distinguishing marks of a holistic theory of atonement?

*First, there are patterns of relationship that can only be described by words like interdependence, inter-relatedness, interconnectedness, interaction.* The words speak for themselves. The universe has been described as 'an immense cohesive continuum';[4] but this definition presupposes a regularity of pattern, a rhythm of life, which, while it can be discerned, does not obscure or deny the aberrations and the contradictions of our world. Patterns of interdependence and interaction do no more than tell of the universal and consistent processes of engagement in which all agencies relate to their mutual advantage or disadvantage. This is one dynamic that appears to be present in all structures and relationships.

These patterns can be observed in our understanding of space and time, in the nature of matter, in the constitution of the atom and the cell, in the processes of evolution. They can be found also in man's relationship with the environment, with his species and with his history. They provide a useful starting point for any consideration of the identity of the individual, his value system, his shared responsibility for the story of the race. 'An inter-relationship exists between all elements and constituents of society. The essential factors in public problems, issues, policies and programmes must always be considered and evaluated as interdependent components of the total system'.[5] The patterns are to be seen again in the dynamics of an international world order, in the insights of holistic medicine, in the creative arts.

*Secondly, these patterns of relationship contain elements of necessity and chance, of spontaneity and choice. There is competition and conflict. There is the appearance of colossal waste.* These elements speak both of the compulsion of circumstance and of the openness to the future. Necessity is the constraining power from without or within that determines – at least in part – the direction in which life moves forward. Chance is not the negative factor that is destructive of developing patterns which have meaning. It is, rather, the possibility that anything might happen. It is the unpredictable bit of life, the random factor, which provides an openness to unforeseen possibilities. There is competition, conflict, and the appearance of waste; but necessity and chance, spontaneity and choice, are the elements that interweave to make the world a 'a kaleidoscope of change'.[6]

The elements of necessity and chance are the complementary principles that secure the spontaneity and the ordered interaction that the evolution of life requires. The element of choice is to be found in the extent to which man can now intervene in the life of his world, maintaining or disturbing the balance of nature to the advantage or disadvantage of all forms of life. The dramatic model of society assumes the necessity of the constraints that are imposed by institutions, by established patterns of behaviour, by the roles that are assigned to all of us as we play our part within the complex web of society; but it also requires the element of chance, or choice, or spontaneity. The awareness of the political and economic interdependence of all people brings with it the possibility that nations might choose to act in the knowledge that the world and the race constitute a single community. Questions of necessity and chance are raised also by our increasing understanding of the extent to which illness can be sparked off by the unresolved anxieties and conflicts of people's lives. The basic principles of a holistic approach to health require the element of choice, the active participation of the patient in his own treatment so that he might bring fully into play his own capacities for self-healing. The inter-play of these elements is to be seen also in all forms of artistic expression. The artist has a choice: he can portray what is required or he can depict what he sees. The true artist will know the compulsion of his art, bearing upon him, drawing him into his work, breaking through to new depths of insight.

*Thirdly, these patterns of relationship are distinguished by a recurring motif of life and death and life. It is the element of sacrifice. It involves an infinite number of unseen deaths – a dying to patterns of independence and self-sufficiency as the part discovers a new identity within the larger purposes of the whole.* A *motif* is the dominant idea of a work. It is in exactly this sense that the *motif* of life and death and life is used here. Sacrifice does not necessarily mean in this context the voluntary act of self-destruction for the sake of some ideal, but it does refer to the importance that must be attached to the *death* which life requires as it moves on. It is only through this process that the complex systems of life achieve their completeness, their wholeness.

The *motif* of life and death and life, is to be found in every area. It is there in the evolution of life. 'The evolution of living forms . . . can only occur when we have entities which are born, which grow, which compete; which then reproduce other entities closely similar to, but not exact copies of themselves; and which then die'.[7] The familiar cycle of birth and growth and activity and death is part of the rhythm of life. There is a pattern of self-renewal as cells break down and build new structures, as tissues and organs replace their cells.[8] The word sacrifice might appear to be inapposite but 'the structures that are constantly being replaced are themselves living organisms. From their point of view the self-renewal of the larger system is their own cycle of birth and death. Birth and death, therefore, now appear as a central aspect of self-organisation, the very essence of life. Indeed, all living things around us renew themselves all the time. . . . But for every organism that dies another is born. Death, then, is not the opposite of life but an essential aspect of it'.[9]

There is a drama of life and death and life to be worked through in man's relationship to his environment. 'An organism that thinks only in terms of its own survival will invariably destroy its environment and will thus destroy itself'.[10] Man's growing self-awareness of his solidarity not only with the environment but with all members of the human race requires a death for attitudes and values and motivations that are destructive of the common good. Interpretations of history can so easily conceal the darkness of the hidden world for which all people have a shared responsibility; but it is only by acknowledging the corporate responsibility for the past and the dynamic this imposes for the future that men and women share creatively in the pattern of life and death and life.

Dying takes a variety of forms. There are crises of transition to be negotiated in life which require a death to established patterns of behaviour. Psychotherapy will often provide the context in which new patterns of life can emerge. Therapeutic centres for the treatment of cancer patients will attempt to explore the psychological and the biological processes. The patient might be required to confront traumas which are making for death and not for life. But death cannot be denied; and it is the achievement of the hospice movement to provide an environment in which the inescapable fact can be admitted and in which there can be a discovery of new life – a wholeness – which transcends the physical process. The artist will know something of this process of transcendence and transformation as new forms of expression and interpretation struggle for recognition. Old art forms are superseded as the creativity of the human imagination breaks out in new ways. It is, perhaps, in the analogy of the Beethoven symphony that we encounter again the pattern of life and death and life as every note retains its place but is caught up in all that has gone before and all that follows after and thus makes its contribution to the whole.

*Fourthly, these patterns of relationship contain the possibility of coherence, the promise of new life.* These things are realised wherever the patterns of interdependence and interaction are managed successfully, wherever the elements of necessity and chance are allowed their appropriate degrees of freedom, wherever the process of life and death and life is worked through.

The integration of electrons and protons, the association of atoms, the organisation of cells all speak of nature's capacity to achieve its patterns of association and coherence. The living world has its ordered hierarchy of systems which continue to evolve. And man's involvement in the total life of the universe requires us to respond to the challenge to see the world as one organism. The interdependence of all forms of life demands an acknowledgement of the wholeness, the at-one-ness, of the world around and within us. There is a tentative but developing awareness of the corporate nature of the life of our species. There are few dominant issues which do not have an international dimension. The challenge that we might learn to live as individuals and as nations who belong to one another and depend upon each other might be represented as another way of speaking about patterns of relationship that contain the possibility of coherence, the promise of new life. The same process is to be found, of course, in the awareness that health relates to the whole person, that health and disease can only be seen in relation to the human organism in its entirety. And the artist, by virtue of his ability to look beyond the familiar and the predictable, to take our immediate concerns and set them within a broader frame of reference, to connect us with the deepest rhythms of life, is able to hint at the possibility of new patterns of understanding which have their own exuberance and integrity.

But is it possible to make connections between our understanding of the world and the insights of Christians theology? *Only One Earth*, the unofficial report commissioned by the Secretary-General of the United Nations Conference on the Human Environment in the early 1970s, concluded its study by bemoaning the lack in earlier generations of a wider rationale of unity. 'Our prophets have sought it, our poets have dreamed it. But it is only in our own day that astronomers, physicists, geologists, chemists, biologists, anthropologists, ethnologists and archaeologists have all combined in a single witness of advanced science to tell us that in every alphabet of our being, we do indeed belong to a single system, powered by a single energy, manifesting a fundamental unity under all its variations, depending for its survival on the balance and health of the total system'.[11]

It has to be asked if the single witness of advanced science is sufficient to provide the vision and the motivation. Could it be that Christian theology can find in the patterns of interdependence and interaction, the elements of necessity and chance, the *motif* of life and death and life, the promise of new life, the framework that will be required for all that must be said about God and man, the reality of evil, the centrality of sacrifice, the meaning of the cross, the experience of death and resurrection, and the hope of an atonement which encompasses all things? Can Christian theology take these things – the common perceptions of knowledge and experience – and use them as the building blocks for that wider rationale of unity which, taking full account of the balance and health of the whole system, is able to transcend it and enable us to find the beginning and the end of our search in God? Is this the meaning of a holistic theory of atonement?

# PART II

# THE TASK OF THEOLOGY

## Chapter 4

# The Task of Theology

Christian theology finds the comprehensive vision, the wider rationale of unity, in the being, the purposes and the activity of God. Christian theology has no monopoly of concern, but the search for wholeness has traditionally found its highest forms of expression in mankind's religious faith. The most primitive forms of religion have been concerned to express and to achieve the desire to have some place in the larger scheme of things, to belong and to be at one. The modern world appears to have lost God. He is no longer required by many to give intelligibility or validation to the experience of life. The prevailing world-view in so many cultures is now dominated by the sciences; but an awareness of the transcendent value of life remains, and there have been pleas for a sense of the wholeness of things because 'we seem to be so constituted that we seek to hold together in a coherent way, in a unified vision which can integrate our existence, all our models of reality – whether from the sciences or from religion'.[1] A unified vision is an essential *sine qua non* for a holistic theory of atonement.

Where does God belong? Is it possible to argue that God alone gives coherence to this sense of wholeness? It is the task of theology to speak about God. It is the task of Christian theology to speak about the God and Father of our Lord Jesus Christ. The patterns of relationship that have been found in so many areas of life do not call in question all that Christian theology is required to say. Theology is informed and enlarged and sharpened by other disciplines. It cannot do its work in isolation. There is a comprehensiveness and a totality about Christian theology which require it to interpret all

31

knowledge and experience in the light of the cross. It remains for those who seek understanding through faith the primary discipline of coherence and interpretation because it finds in God the principle of unity that holds all things together.

The mystery of God's being remains beyond all comprehension. Religious experience is tentative, paradoxical, elusive. Theology bears a deceitful witness to God if it fails to draw attention to its limitations. There comes a point when it can only speak of what it does not know. God reveals Himself as being nearer to me than I am to myself[2]; but He is also the God who is apprehended in the emptiness and the darkness of life, the God who is hidden from our sight, the God who appears to remain silent in response to the cry of pain.

Anthropomorphic images of God can so easily suggest that God can be brought entirely within the range of our experience, defined by our reason and pictured by our imagination. But human rationality is continually confounded by God. The name by which He makes Himself known in the Old Testament – 'I am who I am'[3] – serves to remind us that God is to be found within our experience and yet he remains above and beyond all that can be known and understood. It is one of the constants of religious experience that God eludes us at the precise moment that we dare to believe we have comprehended Him. 'There is in the soul no knowledge of God except the knowledge that it does not know him'.[4]

The mystery that we call God cannot be contained within any word or image or idea. Words, images, ideas – when used in relation to God – are all symbols. Indeed, the word *God* is itself a symbol; but this is precisely the reason why it is possible to speak of God as the supreme symbol of man's search for wholeness. It is here that we begin to find an answer to the question: Why does a unified vision require God? Is God the principle of unity?

It is helpful to recover the origin and the meaning of a *symbol*. 'When two people in ancient Greece made an agreement, they often sealed it by breaking something – a tablet, a ring, a piece of pottery – into two pieces and keeping one half each. If one of these two contracting parties later wanted the bargain honoured, he or his representative would identify himself by fitting his part of the broken object into the other. To "match" was in Greek *symbollein* and the two pieces were called *symbola*.'[5] A symbol is, therefore, something that connects or brings together or makes whole that which is disconnected or fragmented.

Symbols possess great power: a presidential palace, a regimental colour, a wedding ring. It is part of the power of a symbol that it points beyond itself; it hints at a greater truth; it makes connections by virtue of its associations. A symbol can speak of many things. An individual cannot make a symbol. A symbol – if it is to be a living symbol – requires wider recognition. The great symbols of mankind – water and fire – have a range of associations that touch depths in the experience of a generation, a society, a race, or the species as a whole. It is through the use of symbols that men and women are able to give order and coherence and depth and meaning to their lives.

But how do we account for the power of symbols? Is it possible that a symbol might actually participate in what it represents? A symbol can never fully embrace and comprehend the reality of which it speaks. It has been born of it; it shares in it; but it can never possess it. And yet symbols possess great power. They are part of what they signify. Auschwitz has become for recent generations a symbol of evil. The word represents more than the place or the people who were destroyed there. It gathers to itself the torments of the Jewish people, the victims of a systematic policy of genocide of demonic proportions. Its power as a symbol has been determined by the magnitude of their sufferings. Auschwitz – considered as a symbol – is not the reality that it symbolises but it participates in it. The symbol does not merely represent. It has the capacity to participate in the truth that it represents.

Christian theologians recognise the power of the symbols of the Christian religion to participate in the reality of which they speak.[6] They can never be set over and against the truth, the mystery, of which they tell. They bring that truth, that mystery, to life. The truth, the mystery, are present in the symbol.[7] Symbols serve to remind us of the things we do not know and cannot fully express. The words, the images, the ideas of God are symbols that make connections between God and man. They are taken from human experiences and human relationships. They have the power to bring God to life for men and women. They convey – while they live and work – something of the mystery, the being, the activity, the purposes of God. God participates in the symbols and he transcends them. In so far as the symbols are born of our perception of the activity of God, they are God-given symbols.

The great narrative stories of the Old Testament and the great narrative proclamations of the New Testament both provide a theological interpretation of a people's story. They speak of the activity of God in history. They are rich in myth and metaphor and simile and paradox. They are symbolic narratives. Religious language, especially through the use of symbol and myth, finds its own way of interpreting our experience and exploring life's meaning. The myth was used at an early stage in the vocabulary of religious experience, and not least of all in the literature of the ancient near east. It is in the form of myth – and the biblical myths of creation and of the fall are good examples – that the symbols of man's search for meaning find expression. It is an art form that is memorable and complex and subtle. The myths are profoundly true in the sense that they speak of our desire to make sense of our world. They take us beneath the surface of our consciousness. They give expression to the deeper promptings of the human spirit. Myths – like allegories and parables – portray in narrative form the symbols of religious experience and attempt to expound their meaning.

Theology continues to speak of God as the supreme symbol of man's search for wholeness. Religious symbols have lost something of their power for many people. The diversity of religious faith, the contradictions of religious experience, the hatreds that separate the great religious traditions of the world, call in question any idea that God brings together and makes whole that which is disconnected or fragmented. But it is still possible to speak in this way if our experience of God is such that it corresponds with our experience of the world and gives to that experience greater insight and depth of meaning.

The all-important question must then be formulated in this way: Does God enable us to understand the patterns of interdependence and interaction, the elements of necessity and chance, the *motif* of life and death and life, the promise of coherence and new life? Christian theologians speak of these things in different ways. Some will suggest that God alone is able to provide a picture of reality that is comprehensive and coherent.[8] Some will argue that God alone is able to secure our humanity because, if the word *God* should disappear from our vocabulary, man will no longer be required to face the truth of his existence in its unity and totality.[9] Our knowledge of the world demands the comprehensive and coherent picture, the vision of man in his unity and totality. Faith seeking understanding goes beyond the picture and the vision to the dynamic that we call God.

Christian theology is a revealed religion. Its pre-eminent concern is the interpretation of God's revelation in Jesus Christ. Christian theology evolves within the community of faith. This presupposes the activity of the Spirit. 'The word of knowledge – theology – is spoken to *us* before *we* can say it to others'.[10] This is not to grant to revealed theology an indefectibility that it cannot possess. It is in the nature of faith that 'we begin to know, and cease, and begin again'.[11] Theology is required to be rational and reflective, scientific and contemplative. It will be informed by other disciplines but it has its own integrity. The mysteries of revelation are expounded in the great paradoxes of faith, but the propositions of a revealed theology cannot contradict each other. Revealed theology will be mindful of its roots. It will engage critically with the scriptures, with tradition, and with the claims of new learning, experience and conscience. Revealed theology, mindful of the fact that creation is the arena of God's activity, will propose a vision, a way of looking at life, that is sufficiently comprehensive to encompass all knowledge and experience. It will offer its own diagnosis of the human condition. It will be tested by one question: Is it true?

Christian theology is the rational discipline of a revealed

religion. It does not follow, however, that there must be an irreconcilable division between natural and revealed theology, between reason and revelation. Natural theology refuses to rest on tradition or authority alone. It presents the claims of a revealed religion and it draws upon the experience of the world and the interpretation of human reason. It takes its authority from St Paul: 'All that may be known of God by men lies plain before their eyes. . . . His invisible attributes, that is to say his everlasting power and deity, have been visible ever since the world began, to the eye of reason in the things he has made'.[12] Natural theology assumes that the insights of a revealed religion find confirmation in the world. The mind and spirit of man explore the world and attempt to penetrate its mysteries, but the God of revealed and natural theology is discerned by faith and reason in the unfolding drama of history. But can faith and reason correspond? Can revelation and rationality confirm each other? Can the wisdom of God and the wisdom of the world meet in the word of the cross? Is this the measure of the challenge that is posed by a holistic theory of atonement?

It is difficult to distinguish the mystery of God from the symbols and the images by which we speak of Him. One of the perennial problems confronting theology is the need to find appropriate ways of speaking about God. The decline in religious observance, the death of religious symbols, the secularism that pervades so much contemporary thought, present their own challenges. But these specific problems have to be set in a wider context. It is against our understanding of the world that we have to ask if our pictures of God are large enough to contain an expanding universe, the whole drama of evolution, the diversity and energy and rhythm of life. Can they contain the immensity of all that the word *God* must now convey?

The writer of the Letter to the Hebrews insists that those who would draw near to God must believe that He exists and that He rewards those who seek Him.[13] There is no clear picture of the God whom we desire to worship; but Christian orthodoxy may yet prove to be more rich and resourceful than is sometimes supposed. There is no universally accepted proof for the existence of God, but the word is irreplaceable. It touches all the depths.[14] The mystery of God is brought to life by a great variety of pictures. But pictures of God change. A child's kaleidoscope can throw up different pictures with every movement of the hand. Each picture has colour, beauty, order, fascination. So it is that different pictures of God will be thrown up in response to the pressure of new knowledge, new needs. Some pictures will die. They will serve their purpose, but they will eventually outlive their usefulness. They will die and disappear from the consciousness of men and women. Some will remain; but they may be modified, adapted, enlarged. Symbols and myths, images and pictures, speak of the God in whom we live and move and have our being.[15] The symbol, the picture, might provide a way into the mystery of God; but they have their limitations. They are relative. They are partial. The only test that must be applied is whether or not they are still useful. Can we still work with them? Do they express the truth as we see it?

God is known for what He is by what He does. Our images of God will be shaped by our understanding of God's work. The bible tells of the God who acts in history. It is fashionable to look with some misgiving at the anthropomorphic pictures of God: God as king, as judge, as shepherd. These traditional pictures of God, grounded in the scriptures, have provided working models for men and women throughout their lives. It is still possible to recover the original truth of these pictures and to find that it corresponds with things that we need to say in the light of our experience of God and of the world. But there are many for whom these pictures have lost their meaning. It is not merely that they portray an all-too-human God or suggest that God is a remote authority figure. These pictures have their place, but they cannot be the only pictures of God. They will remain, but it is necessary to set them in a large room and find other pictures that can hang beside them.

Pictures of God must attempt to do justice to the immensity of the God of creation and redemption, the God whose purpose is that He shall be all in all. The natural sciences have enlarged our understanding of the world; the human sciences have deepened our understanding of man; both have shown the extent to which we are all bound up in one another. The living world is one organism. All life is one. It is in the light of this knowledge that the insights of the mystics commend themselves. 'Unless a man can find God within himself, in the depths of his own solitude, he will never find him at all. And it may be that until one has found and been transformed by Him there, one will not be able to attain to the vision which enables one to see Him . . . in everything'.[16] This is not to suggest that God is identical with the universe, with the world of nature, with man. God is within and He can still be above and beyond.

The doctrine of creation is a powerful affirmation that life in all its varied forms reveals the activity of God. The doctrine of redemption is a powerful affirmation that God's activity reveals His character and purpose. The doctrines of creation and redemption demand that we take full account of God's relationship with the world, with man in his independence, with evil and suffering. The biblical witness is that God gives Himself to His world. His relationship is one of continuous, creative, passionate, suffering, redeeming and transforming participation. He is the God who comprehends and embraces and is unmistakably part of and who yet over-reaches and over-arches the whole of life. This is the intimacy and the immensity of God. Images of God – old and new – must speak, therefore, of His immanence and His transcendence and they are both bound up together. 'Transcendence means that God has His centre everywhere and His circumference nowhere'.[17]

Different pictures are to be found in the scriptures, in the teachings of the early fathers, in the writings of the mystics. Christian theologians and apologists have been concerned to find some of these pictures and to propose new ones in recent years. There is the picture of God as the fount or source of life from which we flow.[18] This picture has its variations: God as the ocean of which I am a wave; God as the sun of which I am a shaft of light; God as the tree of which I am a branch.[19] These pictures recall Ezekiel's vision of the glory of God coming like the sound of many waters,[20] St Paul's connection between the voice that spoke at creation and the light of the knowledge of the glory of God that is shown in the face of Jesus Christ,[21] and Jesus' analogy of the vine and the branches as one way in which He might speak of His relation with the disciples.[22] These pictures have life and movement. And God and man are seen to belong together. Indeed, the point is made regarding these pictures that the human proceeds from the divine, 'but in such a way that God is present and active in what man is, so that man would simply not be man unless God were so present and active in him'.[23]

A similar emphasis – life coming from life and going back into life – is found also in the picture of God in which His relationship with the creation is compared with the way in which the human mind works within the human body.[24] The picture recalls St Paul's analogy of the church as the body of Christ in which the Lord, who is the head of the body, unites its several parts, so that there might be one body in Him.[25] The picture of God that is taken from our experience of the mind and body has the merit that when we think in these terms – the mind working in and upon the body, and the body working with and for the mind – then we begin to see not merely how God and man can work together, but how the divine can receive the human and give meaning and purpose within a common life and fellowship.[26]

The strength of this insight is picked up and enlarged upon in the picture of God as the cosmic lover.[27] Love gives and receives. Hosea came beyond the heart-break of his marriage to discover the cords of compassion, the bands of love, with which God binds Himself to His people.[28] God's relationship with the world, if it is to be a meaningful relationship, cannot be one-sided. There is a continuing, unbroken interaction. It is in this way that God respects and guarantees the freedom of His creation. God gives and God receives. The world and human history have significance for God. God receives into Himself all that we are and all that we do. The creator and the created, the lover and the beloved, belong together.

It is doubtful if any picture can be preferred to the one that was most beloved by Jesus and that He commended to His disciples – God as Father. It is entirely appropriate to explore all that might be contained within the picture of God as Mother;[29] but the word, the picture, that comes from Jesus is bound to be given pride of place within the Christian tradition. God will continue to transcend all words, images, symbols. He will transcend all personal concepts;[30] but Jesus' picture of God as Father reminds us that man's story is inescapably bound up with God's story. The word *God* remains. 'It exists. It comes from those origins from which man himself comes. Its demise can be thought of only along with the death of man himself. It can still have a history whose changing forms we cannot imagine in advance, precisely because it is what keeps an uncontrollable and unplanned future open. It is our opening to the incomprehensible mystery'.[31]

The mystery is inseparable from the search for wholeness. It is encountered in the diversities of experience. It is received in faith. It provides its own meaning. It makes its own demands. Beyond the arguments of reason, the fabrications of the human mind, there are the claims of love. 'The true science of God is that which leads us to love God'.[32] The word, the picture, the pattern of Jesus is decisive for Christian theology. It is in the obedience of love that we discover the truth of God and receive some glimpse of the meaning of atonement.

*Chapter 5*

# God and Man

God is God. But man's knowledge of God cannot be separated from his knowledge of himself. Man's search for God is bound up with his search for himself. And the widest possible interpretation that might be placed upon God's purposes does not diminish the role that appears to have been assigned to man. Man's unique capacity to question, to interpret and to articulate makes it necessary to examine more closely God's relation to man.

The search for new images of God has been determined in part by the desire to find appropriate ways of speaking of God's relation to the world. The Christian doctrine of *creatio ex nihilo* affirms that all things have their origin in God. The story of God goes far beyond the story of man. The first biblical myth affirms that 'God saw everything that He had made, and behold, it was very good'.[1] The whole created order comes within the providence of God. Creation is the work of grace.

But what does creation tell us about the sovereignty and the purposes of God? Is creation something that is external to God except in so far as He is ultimately responsible for the work of His hands? Or is it, perhaps, fundamental to His sovereignty and His purposes – inextricably bound up with the mystery of His eternal being – that there is to be found in His relation to His creation the patterns of interdependence and interaction, the elements of necessity and chance, the *motif* of life and death and life, the promise of new life, that can be traced throughout the living world?

One helpful analogy has been taken from our experience of life to illuminate the nature of God's relation to the world.

'The concept of God as Creator has, in the past, been too much dominated by a stress on the externality of God's creative acts – He is regarded as creating something external to Himself, just as the male fertilises the womb from the outside. But mammalian females, at least, create within themselves and the growing embryo resides within the female body and this is a proper corrective to the masculine picture – it is an analogy of God creating the world within herself, we would have to say.'[2] The analogy should not be pressed too far. It is necessary to be reminded that, although for the mother, the foetus is in some sense flesh of her flesh, growth continues until the time when there are two distinct entities.[3] The analogy must not be pursued to the point where it leads either to a cosmic dualism or to a sense that the creation can ever become independent of its creator. The picture does no more than speak of the belief that creation is God's act within Himself.

The picture of transcendence and immanence that has been presented in which both are bound up in each other demands that we find the narrow path that leads between a deism that affirms the divine act of creation but denies God's continuing activity in the world and a pantheism in which God is identified with the creation. This path leads to a panentheistic view which holds transcendence and immanence in a creative tension, emphasising God's participation in the world to the point where it might be said that everything is in God and yet maintaining the absolute sovereignty of God who continues to stand over and beyond His creation. Transcendence and immanence can then be seen as concepts that are interlocking and mutually enriching. What is being described is a process, a relationship, of continuous interaction between God and the world; a process, a relationship, that might be likened to the activity of the cells in relation to the organism, of man in relation to society, of the artist in relation to his age. But any exploration of this process is bound to take account of man's self-awareness, freedom and power.

One helpful illustration of the meaning of our self-awareness is provided by Jung's account of his visit to the Athai plains of Kenya in 1925. He looked out over the great game preserve. He separated himself from his travelling companions and entered the silence of the place and brought his own self-consciousness to bear upon it. It was there that he saw with such clarity what he called the cosmic meaning of consciousness. Man is necessary for the completion of creation because he brings to the world his awareness of its objective existence and meaning.[4] Is this the significance of our self-awareness? Is this the part that only man can play? We are participants and observers and interpreters. Is it one of our distinctive characteristics that we alone can make explicit the things that we see around us, that we can bring into the continuing drama of creation our conscious awareness of life?

But man's self-awareness cannot be considered apart from his freedom. God gives to the creation its own freedom. This is not to claim either for the created order in general or for man in particular a greater degree of autonomy than they actually possess. The relationship is one of interdependence, but there is a freedom – at least for man – which has its origin in God and in His will for the creation. Man is part of that whole process of being and belonging and behaving and becoming which, although it is circumscribed in so many ways, is still a reflection of God's eternal freedom.

Man possesses the freedom to create and to destroy, to love and to hate, to heal and to hurt. But what is the extent of our independence? Is it possible to insist that nothing is outside God and yet to insist that man is truly free? There is a paradox at the heart of the biblical doctrine of creation. It affirms that all life has its origin in God, that nothing has a prior or independent existence; and yet it points to the creation of forms of life that exist in some sense over and against God.[5] It is significant that the biblical myths of creation and of the fall stand alongside each other. They require each other if they are to speak of man's continuing experience. The sovereign act of creation does not exclude the elements of necessity and chance. The goodness of creation encompasses the fact of competition and conflict. The wonder of creation stands alongside the appearance of colossal waste. The at-one-ness of life does not deny the experience of alienation.

The fall is not merely an ingredient of every moment of every individual life but of all life. Sin is not only personal. It is cultural and corporate. It is a condition of life that God permits and respects the autonomy that He gives to His creation; and not merely permits and respects it; but takes account of it and accepts its consequences for man, for the created order, and ultimately for Himself.

But the connections continue. Man's self-awareness cannot be considered apart from his freedom. His freedom cannot be considered apart from his power. Man is part of creation, and yet he stands in his self-awareness and his freedom over and above the created order. He shares his biological needs with the animal creation; and yet he has the power to subdue the earth and possess it,[6] to determine the direction in which society and his own species and the environment of all living things shall develop. We are brought back to our understanding of chance as the possibility that anything might happen. This is the freedom and the power that God gives to His creation. This is the nature of His relation to the world and to man in his independence that 'God makes the world make itself; or rather, since the world is not a single being, He makes the multitude of created forms make the world, in the process of making or being themselves'.[7]

And yet man is man and not God. We have to come to terms with our own mortality. The search for wholeness which is inseparable from the search for meaning is born of the self-awareness, the freedom and the power that we possess. We have our awareness of the world around us. We have the freedom to push back the boundaries and explore the unknown possibilities. We have the power to shape our destiny. But we cannot escape the questions about ultimate meaning. We find that our story is bound up with God's story, and it is exactly here that we encounter the truth of our existence which is the truth about God and man.

It is essential to return, therefore, to the need to see life in its entirety, to the wider rationale of unity, to the comprehensive vision. But what are the consequences for our understanding of God of all that has been said about man in his self-awareness, his freedom and his power? What are the corresponding characteristics that God displays as we encounter Him in His relation with the world, with human history, with the lives of nations and of individuals? There are no direct counterparts, but – taken in the round – the characteristics that have been identified in man speak of the self-limitation, the self-emptying and the active participation of God.

God's self-limitation and self-emptying are not a theological device for coming to terms with the fact that God has created the world in such a way that He cannot or will not intervene. God does not withdraw. The patterns of engagement are too well established, too easily discerned. There is a balance in the relationship, a creative tension, which makes for order and not for chaos, for life and not for death. God's providential care involves divine initiative and divine intervention. 'It is this principle of divine action that gives the world such endless vitality, such vital vitality in every part'.[8]

It is customary to speak of God's self-emptying in relation to the incarnation, but the incarnation cannot be separated from the continuing and unbroken activity of creation and redemption. The self-limitation, the self-emptying, the self-giving of God are seen in His sovereign act of creation; namely, that it is His will that there shall be created beings who stand alongside Him or even, perhaps, over against Him. The whole thrust of the biblical story is of God going out of Himself, calling to Himself a people with whom He establishes a covenant relationship, enabling His purposes to be discerned in the events of history but guaranteeing the freedom of man to respond or to withdraw. The great biblical themes of grace, of creation, of election, of covenant, of revelation, of redemption speak of the God who gives Himself to His creation. God exercises His sovereignty in such a way that He puts Himself at risk. Creation, incarnation and redemption belong together. The self-limitation and self-emptying speak of the humility and the patience, the suffering and the sacrifice of God.

God wills to be known but He works within the constraints of His creation. His participation in the world does not deny the autonomy of the creation. His sovereignty and His purposes are worked out in relation to man's freedom. The relationship involves His active participation. There are urgent questions that have to be considered with regard to the experience of evil but the Christian doctrine of creation affirms that ultimately all life is from God and cannot be seen apart from Him. It is only in the light of this conviction that the mystical tradition sees the whole creation being grounded in God: 'every atom and electron, every living cell and organism, every plant and animal, every human being exists for ever in this eternal being'.[9] So comprehensive is this vision of God in his relation to the world that Jung, standing on the boundaries of the Christian tradition, speaks of creation as 'only the first commitment in a continuing act of creation wherein all life participates every second of night and day'.[10] Is this the point to which we have been brought? Is this the comprehensive vision that unites all knowledge and experience in God? Is this the truth about God and man: the participation of all life in the light of God's first and continuing commitment? The God and Father of us all, who is above all and through all and in all,[11] remains transcendent and immanent, and pursues His purposes of love in a relationship of free participation.

# Chapter 6

# God and Evil

It is the experience of evil that obscures the picture of God as the symbol of man's search for wholeness. Christian theology speaks of the God who takes account of the autonomy He gives to His creation and argues that He accepts its consequences for man, for the created order, and ultimately for Himself. But the experience of evil and of suffering continues to question the reality of God, His power and His love. It is appropriate that the biblical myths of creation and of the fall should stand alongside each other, but their common witness to man's search for meaning cannot conceal the darkness and the torment of the human predicament. If the doctrine of *creatio ex nihilo* is concerned to affirm that all things have their origin in God, then the fact of evil cries out for explanation. God's sovereignty must take account of destructive conflict, of colossal waste, of alienation, of the fact of death. Ancient myths tell of the experience of evil – the conflict, the temptation, the capacity for self-destruction – but unless we are prepared to find the explanation in a cosmic dualism and posit the existence of an independent force that is eternally and irreconcilably opposed to God, questions concerning the origin of evil continue to press themselves upon us.

Does evil find its origin in God? It is a commonplace to suggest that evil and suffering are implicit in the act of creation, that God permits evil and suffering and is ultimately responsible for them. Christian orthodoxy has always claimed that God lives with evil, wrestles with evil, conquers evil. This is part of His pain and His passion. Some would suggest however that this does not take us far enough. Eastern religions have emphasised the necessity of reconciling within

47

God the ambiguities of our experience. Good and evil appear to belong together. Do the everyday illustrations that can be taken from life suggest that good and evil are fundamentally inseparable? It is the impurities in the atmosphere that make it possible for the human eye to delight in a magnificent sunset. It is the temper tantrums of a young child which contain the possibility that the mature adult will have an independent mind and spirit. It is the divine madness that has tormented artists even to the point of self-destruction that has made it possible for them to accomplish works of incomparable beauty and originality. If all life has its origin in God, is it possible to argue that there is evil *in* God. Isaiah speaks of the God who creates light and darkness, who makes weal and woe.[1] And this theme was picked up by Jacob Boehme, the seventeenth century German Protestant mystic, who insisted that because 'God is all', He must therefore be light and darkness, love and wrath.[2] This was for Boehme a necessary part of God's self-disclosure, the means whereby we achieve understanding.[3]

A similar approach to the problem of evil has been adopted by Jung. It was for a him a cause of great anxiety that Christian orthodoxy had diminished the totality of God by excluding evil from the divine being. Indeed, it was the exclusion of evil from God which had led in his judgement to the representation of the dark side of our experience by the mythical figure of Satan. The opposites of good and evil, which he considered to be essential for completeness, must be located within God if He is to represent the totality of being.[4] It was not sufficient for Jung to speak of God as love. He needed to set alongside conventional piety his strong sense that somewhere and somehow God was terrible and stood in a relationship with evil and used it as an instrument of reconciliation.[5]

Grace Jantzen, proceeding from the premise that all things have their origin in God, urges the need to reflect again upon Boehme's insights. She argues that the conflict between light and darkness, between good and evil, can only have its origin in God and must, therefore, be in some sense, a reflection of Him.[6] Her picture of the world as God's body is pressed to the point where she argues that the evil we find in the world appears to be evil in God.[7]

But Christian orthodoxy has never been able to accommodate the notion that good and evil belong together, that evil has its origin in God. And yet the questions persist: How does God reconcile Himself and His creation to the evil and the suffering that exist? What is God's guarantee that all things work together for good in a world that He has made? Something has been said concerning the importance of symbol and myth, the appropriateness of picture language, if we are to speak of God. Is there some contemporary symbol or picture that might be used as these questions are pursued?

A second approach to the problem of evil is also prompted by Jung's work. In the course of his journey into his own unconscious, Jung encountered what he called the *shadow*. The shadow is the other self, the hidden self, the unacceptable and unwanted part of the truth about ourselves. But the shadow contains creative elements that are required for personal maturity, and its denial leads to distortion and destruction. Wholeness can only be achieved by a resolution, a reconciliation, of the conscious self and the shadow.[8]

It is tempting to suggest that it might be helpful to a contemporary understanding of the problem of evil to portray evil as the shadow in God's creation, the shadow with which God is required to live and with which He must be reconciled, because it is within His creation and, therefore, within Himself. Is it part of the self-limitation, the self-emptying, the active participation of God that He must contain the shadow within His creation? Is it part of the sacrifice of God that He must bear all the tensions until at a moment of His choosing there is a cosmic act of reconciliation?

These approaches to the questions surrounding the experience of evil cannot be allowed to stand uncontested. The concept of evil being in God does remove any possibility of a cosmic dualism. The picture of evil as the shadow in God's creation can provide a way of illustrating how good and evil live side by side until God's act of reconciliation releases the energies of the new creation. It might be possible to speculate in either of these ways but for the fact that our generation has at its disposal in the literature of the holocaust a *corpus* of experience which removes any doubt concerning the reality of evil, its relationship to God, its utterly demonic character.

Few people have done more than Elie Wiesel to make us face the truth of the holocaust. He was taken as a boy of fourteen to Auschwitz. He saw the evil of the place and found that everything recoiled within him. He gives his own horrendous commentary upon that experience: 'Never shall I forget that night, the first night in camp, which has turned my life into one long night, seven times cursed and seven times sealed. Never shall I forget that smoke. Never shall I forget the little faces of the children, whose bodies I saw turned into wreaths of smoke beneath a silent sky. Never shall I forget those flames which consumed my faith for ever. Never shall I forget that nocturnal silence which deprived me, for all eternity, of the desire to live. Never shall I forget those moments which murdered my God and my soul, and turned my dreams to dust. Never shall I forget these things, even if I am condemned to live as long as God Himself. Never.'[9]

Do good and evil belong together? Does evil have its origin in God? Is evil the shadow in God's creation? The suffering of a single person that defies all reasonable explanation cries out to be heard. The experiences of the holocaust, which sharpen the urgency with which the questions surrounding evil present themselves, remove these questions from the area of discussion as speculations that are deeply offensive to all that Christian thought and experience mean by God.

Is it, therefore, possible to speak of evil as an autonomous force that is irreconcilably opposed to God without conceding the claims of a cosmic dualism? One significant treatment in recent generations has been Karl Barth's exposition of the stubborn element in creation which he has termed *Nothingness*.[10] It is not nothing. It is *Nothingness*. Barth denies emphatically that this alien factor exists in God, or that it might even be considered as the negative aspect or the shadowy side of creation. It is the principle of total enmity. It is the source of corruption and death. It is utterly opposed to God and to all His work. There is no dualism in Barth's theology. *Nothingness* is not another god. It is not self-created. 'It is purely and simply what God did not, does not and cannot will'.[11]

The first creation myth speaks of the darkness upon the face of the deep.[12] It is here in the darkness, in the nothingness of the chaos, that Barth locates 'the reality behind God's back'.[13] The contention that there is an inherent contradiction in God's creation is self-evident. It has still to be asked, however, if it is permissible to take one word from a creation myth and invest it with so much meaning. The concept of *Nothingness* gives us a way of holding fast to the sovereignty of God, of admitting the reality of evil as the impossible possibility, and yet of asserting the ultimate victory of God who alone is able to comprehend, to control and to conquer.[14] *Nothingness* is evil. It has its own being, existence and form. It is the utter negation of grace and Barth will only consider it in the context of grace. It is in God's decisive act of revelation and redemption in Jesus Christ that all the questions surrounding evil are seriously raised and seriously answered.[15]

No theological interpretation of history is able to ignore evil. It is a universal phenomenon. It is the demonic power which runs riot throughout the created order. It violates and destroys life. It cannot be confused with the potentially creative elements that exist within the depths of our personal or corporate shadow. It is the utterly negative and destructive force at work at the deepest level in the fabric of all life which cannot be transformed. Our personal experience of evil and suffering – perplexing and tormenting – can only be an infinitesimally small part of something that goes beyond the imagination, transcending our experience as a race. Evil is in history and it is beyond history. We are compelled to recognise that evil is inseparable from creation. Its origins appear to lie in the freedom which God gives to His creation.

Paul Tillich uses the word *estrangement* to speak of the universal predicament. It is not a biblical word, although the theme of estrangement is found throughout the bible. It is an appropriate word because it carries the implication that we are separated from that to which essentially we belong.[16] Man's self-awareness leads him to some understanding of his estrangement from God who is the ground of his being. Creation and the fall are inseparable but they have a wider frame of reference than man. Tillich rejects any suggestion that there was ever a moment in time when man and nature were changed from good to evil.[17] 'Actualised creation' and 'estranged existence' belong together.[18] Evil is 'the structure of self-destruction' which is fundamental to the state of universal estrangement which encompasses the whole creation.[19]

Man is estranged from his own kind – his species, his race, his fellows. Tillich brings together in his argument 'tragic destiny' and 'moral freedom'.[20] The element of tragic destiny represents the pressures from without. It has the force of necessity. It speaks of the universal fall. Biological, psychological and sociological influences inform every decision. The pattern of interdependence persists. Man cannot be isolated from the structures and the network of social relationships that are permeated by evil. And so it is that all life is continuously present: 'the universe participates in every act of human freedom'.[21] But moral freedom remains. It is the element of chance, of choice. Man's freedom is grounded in the fact of his creation in the image of God. Moral freedom represents man's individual responsibility. God respects man's freedom and works with it but the gift of freedom exposes us to the ravages of evil. 'Sin is a universal fall before it becomes an individual act'.[22] Estrangement is not a word that can be used as a substitute for sin. The temptation is to be like God.[23] Sin is love that has turned from God to self.[24] It is the act by which man takes to himself and explores and enlarges the predicament of estrangement. Estrangement leads to destruction and despair. It is the abandonment of all search for meaning, the loss of hope.

It is despair that brings to the forefront of our awareness the measure of the problem that is posed by evil. The human predicament is incomprehensible. There is a common inheritance of guilt. Man is vulnerable, culpable and impotent. There are so many situations in which 'man is not only an executioner, not only a victim, not only a spectator: he is all three at once'.[25] And the evil in which we share is irrecoverable. There is a place in the scheme of things for the act of confession, the gift of forgiveness, the healing of broken relationships, the expression of good intentions for the future. But evil cannot be recalled; it has gone forth; it is.

It is the task of theology to insist that God alone is able to provide the one truly coherent and comprehensive picture of reality, that God alone is able to demand that man shall see himself in his unity and totality. To abandon God – to lose sight of God – is to find that the picture is distorted, that our humanity is placed in jeopardy. Evil and suffering bring into sharp focus all the questions we want to ask about God and man: 'who God and we are, and what God and we can do and have done'.[26] They are questions that cannot be answered. Myths and symbols bring evil within our cognisance, but it remains beyond our understanding. It is the grotesque, inescapable, God-denying, life-destroying fact. Theories can so easily diminish its reality because they purport to make intelligible that which defies all rational explanation. Evil cannot be accommodated in this way. All logical propositions, all poetic images, are inadequate and anything which renders evil manageable for man denies its truth.

God's relationship with evil continues to perplex. God cannot be the symbol of man's search for wholeness if the experience of evil remains outside His dealings with the world. The alien factor, the tragic destiny, must be taken up by God into His pattern of creation, incarnation, redemption and transformation. The silence of Job remains. It is the true response of faith and hope. It is possible in the silence to acknowledge our impotence in the face of evil.

*Chapter 7*

# The Triune God

A holistic theory of atonement does not merely proceed from an understanding of the world but from an encounter with the living God. Christian theology, which is the theology of the God who reveals Himself in action in His world, finds its most distinctive and potent picture of the Godhead in its Trinitarian faith.

The mystery of God's being remains beyond all comprehension, but what He allows us to apprehend must be consistent with what He is in the fullness of His being. The starting-point for the development of Trinitarian faith is Christology, but the bible bears a comprehensive witness to the Triune God. It is within the drama of salvation history, which is the interpreted experience of the people of God, that the gradual unfolding of Trinitarian faith can be traced. It is the abiding significance of Trinitarian faith that it holds in a living tension the church's experience of Jesus and of the Holy Spirit with its absolute conviction in the unity of the Godhead. God is Himself 'the content of His revelation through the Son and in the Spirit'.[1]

Trinitarian faith speaks of 'eternal distinctions and internal relations in the Godhead as wholly and mutually interpenetrating one another in the one identical perfect being of the Father, Son and Holy Spirit'.[2] But the complexities of Trinitarian theology should not obscure the one necessary contention that what we are given in Trinitarian faith is a holistic model of God. 'The doctrine of the Trinity is designed to secure and interpret God's sovereignty in every direction'.[3] Trinitarian faith speaks of the mystery, the unity and the activity of God. It takes seriously the range of human experience. It provides a theological interpretation of history. It encapsulates all that the church must say about God and His relation to the world, to man in his independence, and to evil and suffering. It speaks of the God who acts. It provides one of the essential elements of continuity in Christian thought.

Nothing less than a holistic model of God will be sufficient for a holistic theory of atonement. The patterns of association that have been identified in the living world have been referred to as patterns of at-one-ness. These patterns have four distinguishing characteristics – patterns of interdependence and interaction, elements of necessity and chance, the *motif* of life and death and life, and the promise of new life. But these patterns of at-one-ness can only be identified as signs of the atonement that God has accomplished in the death and resurrection of Jesus if these characteristics have their origin in God.

No claim can be advanced for any theory of atonement unless it proceeds from our understanding of God. A holistic theory of atonement, although it might draw upon a holistic understanding of the world with its complex patterns of relationships, will only have integrity if it can be demonstrated that God's work of creation and redemption is carried forward in these ways – on the basis of these four propositions – because this is how God is and how God chooses to act. Our models of God, our models of atonement, must have rationality and coherence. The wisdom of God and the wisdom of the world can meet in the word of the cross if it can be shown that the distinguishing characteristics of the patterns of at-one-ness in the living world are the distinguishing characteristics of the divine life which Christian theology has identified as Father, Son and Holy Spirit, three Persons and one God. It is only on this basis that the claim can be sustained that 'the Trinity is the key to a religious understanding of the universe'.[4]

First, the patterns of interdependence and interaction are so well attested that it is impossible to avoid the conclusion that if creation has any meaning it requires us to say that 'in this one world, in order that it shall be one, each thing must necessarily exist for all else and all else for each thing'.[5] Is there to be found here some insight into the life of the Divine Trinity?

Christian theology asserts that God is 'the One in three ways of being'.[6] But it does not speak of three persons in some amorphous and undifferentiated unity; nor of three persons who are independent and diversified in their essential nature and being. There is in the Godhead an identity of being and an identity of purpose. There is, both within the divine life and within God's relationship with His creation, that degree of penetrating interdependence that is reflected in the whole of life. 'What is involved is the *one* work of the *One* God, but the one work that is moved within itself'.[7]

Secondly, the the elements of necessity and chance speak of the tension that exists within our experience, of the destiny that is imposed from without or within, and of the freedom to explore unimaginable possibilities. It is not only within man that these elements can be discerned; but if man is made in the image of God, if the creation reflects – and can only reflect – the being of God, is there to be found here also some insight into the life and activity of the Divine Trinity?

The destiny and freedom of the divine life are to be found both within the purposefulness that makes for order and not for chaos, and in the self-emptying in which God gives Himself to His creation in love. Only those who are free can give freedom to others. Only those who have power can give power to others. Only those who love can give and receive in love. It is precisely for this reason that new pictures can speak so meaningfully of the divine life giving and receiving, drawing into Himself all that we are and do. It is this conviction that affords some awareness of the necessity and the chance, of the giving and the receiving, of the love, of the life, in which the Father, the Son and the Holy Spirit continually abide.

Thirdly, the *motif* of life and death and life is found throughout the created order as the cycle of birth and growth and activity and decline and death occurs and repeats itself. Is it possible that this *motif* can be found within the being of God? Is the inescapable fact of death to be seen within the Godhead? Does sacrifice begin and end in God?

The early church took as its starting-point for the development of Trinitarian faith its experience of God in Jesus Christ. It is in the cross that the rationality of the world and the rationality of God meet and become one. 'The Almighty exists and acts and speaks here in the form of One who is weak and impotent, the Eternal as One who is temporal and perishing. . . . The One who lives for ever has fallen a prey to death. The Creator is subjected to and overcome by the onslaught of that which is not'.[8] The mystery of the cross points beyond the crucifixion of the Son to the mystery of the divine life. Nothing can remain outside God. The *motif* is one of life and death *and life*. 'In the death of Jesus Christ God's "Yes", which constitutes all being, exposed itself to the "No" of the nothing. In the resurrection of Jesus Christ this "Yes" prevailed over the "No" of the nothing.'[9]

Fourthly, the promise of new life brings together the holistic model of God and the holistic theory of atonement. Karl Rahner's judgement that 'the Trinity is a mystery of *salvation*'[10] derives from the personal and corporate life of Christian experience. Trinitarian faith commends itself on the basis of what God has done and is doing with and through His people. 'Salvation is fulfilment, the supreme, sufficient, definitive and indestructible fulfilment of being'.[11]. This is the possibility of coherence, the promise of new life, which is contained within the Christian hope. This fourth proposition, this God-given principle of life, does not only speak of the inexhaustible depths and riches of the divine life. It tells of God's desire to go out and to draw into Himself for His eternity the created world, redeemed and restored. It is the promise to make all things new.

It is this promise which leads us on to one final consideration. The use of the word *person* in relation to the Trinity can only be understood in its original sense as the mask worn by an actor to signify the dramatic parts he was playing. It comes to us from the theatre. The mask concealed the features of the actor but his voice could still be heard. All words, images and symbols fail to express the fullness of the God who reveals Himself in three modes of being. He reveals Himself but the mystery transcends our experience. He is the

God whose face cannot be seen,[12] the God who dwells in unapproachable light.[13]

The dramatic image is instructive. Good theatre involves the audience. The actors do not play to an empty house. The interaction between the players and the audience is a vital ingredient. We are not passive spectators. The good actors capture our attention, our imagination, our feelings. They take us with them and draw us into their interpretation of the drama. Thus it is that Daniélou speaks of the Trinity as the essence of Christianity: 'For Christianity is the appeal addressed to man by the Father inviting him to share in the life of the Son through the gift of the Spirit'.[14] The invitation that is contained within the dramatic model of the Triune God speaks of nothing less than our participation in the divine life. The will of God is that man shall be at one with the ground and centre of all being.

But the dramatic model is also the holistic model. The Christian hope extends beyond God's will for the human species. The plan for the fullness of time is that *all things* shall be united in Christ.[15] The question that has already been asked concerning the specific contribution man is able to make by virtue of his self-awareness takes on a new importance. We are able to bring to consciousness all that we see around us. Is this some small part of our distinctive contribution as a race to the continuing drama of God's creation and redemption? To speak of our participation in the divine life is to give expression to the conviction that all life shall be drawn into the divine life.

This is an idea that is consistent with the insights of the scriptures. The holistic model of God and the holistic theory of atonement both speak of the cosmic dimension that will not be obscured by the emphasis that has been placed upon man's special destiny. There is no exclusive privilege that attaches to the ability to comprehend unless it is the capacity to keep open for others the possibilities of which we have so little understanding. This is the one qualification that must be made as we move beyond all images and symbols and try to catch something of the meaning of the insights of the mystics that 'to comprehend and understand God above all similitude, such as He is in Himself, is to be God with God'.[16] It is an ancient theme. The purposes of God transcend the deepest meaning that we can give to life. The theologians of the Greek church have always had a way of speaking about the Christian hope which can properly be called at-one-ment. It is nothing less than the deification of man through participation in the life of the Holy Trinity.

# PART III

# THE MEANING OF SACRIFICE

## Chapter 8

# Ancient Rites

The relationship of the cross to the hope of atonement requires some clear acknowledgement of the place of sacrifice within the Christian understanding of God's self-revelation in Jesus Christ. The patterns of at-one-ness within the world at large suggest a recurring *motif* of life and death and life. This is the natural process through which all the constituent parts of the created order – including man – must pass. But this *motif* implies far more than a process which merely repeats itself. It is the presence within this pattern of the element of sacrifice which releases the power, the energy, which makes for the renewal of life and the promise of new life.

Sacrifice has always been inseparable from man's religious experience and expression. It constitutes an important part of man's response to his world. It was through sacrifice that primitive man attempted to give meaning to his world and achieve some sense of participation in the forces of life, even in the life of God Himself. The ancient world with its long since abandoned rituals of sacrifice invites us to go into the darkness of our experience as a race, to penetrate our corporate unconscious, to enter a world of basic human drives and dependencies.

Sacrifice was widely practised and it has been widely interpreted. There is no one theory that can make sense of the great variety of sacrifices known to anthropologists. It is necessary to guard against theories of sacrifice which suggest a degree of intelligibility, sophistication and comprehensiveness which early rituals did not possess. Sacrificial rites expressed for primitive man the same fundamental search for meaning, identity and coherence that more sophisticated theological systems and liturgical patterns have expressed for the developed religions of the world.

There is no evidence to suggest that the rituals evolved from one primitive pattern. It is sufficient to acknowledge that sacrifice had a central place in many cultures throughout the world, and that rituals contained dimensions that are of anthropological, historical and psychological importance. The sacrifices were related to the rhythms of nature and of the life of man and of the community. It is impossible to dismiss these ancient rites as phenomena that belong to an earlier phase in the evolutionary cycle from which nothing can now be learned. It may well be that there are insights, symbolic actions, experiences, in all these things which connect the contemporary world not only with the rhythms of life but with the being and purposes of God.

Sacrifice has been a significant word in the church's theological vocabulary from the beginning. The world of Christian theology – rational, interpretative, critical – is far removed from the world of primitive sacrificial rites. There are important connections that can be made, but in attempting to understand these ancient rites we are leaving behind the world of the mind and entering the world of primary human needs and feelings – the need for food, for the fertility of man and beast, for the preservation of life, for fellowship, for protection from famine and disease and death. For individuals and for communities, the ritual provided some kind of security in situations in which man was forced to recognise that he was alone and vulnerable.

Sacrifices can only be understood in their local setting. The ritual was an art-form in which the element of celebration was often dominant. Sacrifices were frequently accompanied by ritual chants, by loud cries, by the noise of musical instruments, by dancing. They were often bound up with the life-story of a people. The communal dimension was significant. The ritual dramatised fundamental myths and beliefs and values. Some symbols possess a universal meaning, but rituals and symbols cannot be fully understood except by reference to the culture to which they belong.

One recent interpretation suggests that sacrificial ritual was the means whereby primitive societies contained the violence that is endemic in human relationships.[1] The victim, who stood as a substitute or surrogate for either a person or the community and whose destruction lay at the heart of the sacrificial rite, provided the means whereby violence was deployed to protect the community from the violence that would destroy its life. The myths and rituals of primitive societies recalled and reproduced the events in which all these things had their origin. But it is quite impossible to accommodate all known rituals in this way within one comprehensive theory concerning the nature of primitive religion. It is sufficient to recognise that the ritual often re-enacted the circumstances in which the community came into existence. It was, therefore, able to provide links for the community with its past, its present and its future.

The claims of the community as a whole upon its members derived from the fact that, 'Ancient society was a single unit. . . . The memory, habits, beliefs, feelings are racial. . . . The span of life is that of the race, the community, not of the individual members of it. . . . Every community is a whole, and acts as a whole for all purposes'.[2] The life of the community found its most distinctive and creative expression in sacrifice. The rituals which followed established and elaborate patterns of procedure did not merely give voice to the aspirations of the community, they provided a means of articulating and managing and renewing the social order, the social relations and the social values.

Two theories have traditionally dominated the debate concerning the function of sacrifice. The first suggests that sacrifices should be considered primarily as gifts that were offered to a deity in order to secure some special benefit. The second urges that sacrifices are to be seen above everything else as a communion rite, a means of feasting on and with the deity. These two theories are not mutually exclusive. Nor do they conflict with another interpretation which suggests that the overriding purpose served by sacrifice was the maintenance and the renewal of life. It is recognised that the sacrificial ritual was related to man's basic dependency needs. It was the means whereby primitive man attempted to manage and control the uncertain and the unpredictable aspects of his experience. It is recognised also that sacrificial rituals belong to the life of the community. It dramatised its myths. It gave expression to its values. It renewed the social order. There is, therefore, this third strand in the ancient rites – the maintenance and the renewal of life – that must be identified.

Primitive man had an awareness of the inter-relatedness of life. There were no arbitrary distinctions between man and the animal creation and inanimate objects. One life ran through all things. There was a wholeness about creation, and man participated in all that surrounded him by living simultaneously in the seen and the unseen world.[3] Sacrifice deepened a community's awareness of the mystery of things. It provided the means whereby connections could be made with the fundamental forces that inhabited the world. It made the link between two worlds. It established some form of communication between the sacred and the profane. But these things could only happen because sacrifice was the established means of bringing into play for the advantage of the community the power that renews and makes whole. F. W. Dillistone suggests that according to the literature of the Brahmanas in India 'sacrifice is . . . the power that makes the world go round'.[4] It was through the offering of sacrifice that unity and continuity might be maintained, that death might lead to life.

It is scarcely possible to recapture the simplicity of the earliest rites and all that they represented. Sacrifice was a feature of the life of the early Semitic nomads, preceding the establishment of settled communities, the provision of sacred buildings, and the ordering of a regular cultus. Certain places took on a special character. Certain rocks or trees assumed a special significance. Grain might be scattered. Oil might be poured. An animal might be sacrificed. The sacrifice might be an act of thanksgiving or communion. It might be offered by an individual, a family, a community. In different ways and at different times, the basic needs and dependencies were given expression as man participated in the vital forces of life.

It is difficult to exaggerate the importance of the blood sacrifice in primitive religions. Great significance was attached to blood, and the process of passing from death to life within the sacrificial ritual was believed to establish a relationship with the supernatural order and renew the life forces. Archaeological evidence suggests that blood sacrifices have an ancient pedigree. Cave paintings which depict scenes of wounded animals and masked dancers, the widespread use of blood or of red ochre in the decoration of sacred objects in the cult of the dead, all confirm that for many primitive societies life was believed to reside in the blood of man and beast alike. The symbolism of blood appears to have had a universal appeal, and Dillistone suggests that its origin might well be found in the precariousness of life in which 'the all-important possession is *life* itself. . . . And of all the manifestations of life none is more sacred or more treasured than blood. All the members of a tribe share the same blood. Blood-revenge, blood-ceremonies, blood-covenants are of intense significance in nomadic life. When blood is taken, blood must be restored'.[5]

What is reflected here is something even more fundamental than man's need to hunt and kill in order to survive. The life is in the blood. The shedding of blood was associated with the loss of vitality, and many have therefore inferred that primitive man associated the offering of blood sacrifices with the renewal of life. 'From all parts of the world evidence has been gathered to show that the essential pattern of offering an object containing or representing life to pass through a process actualising or symbolising death in order to sustain and increase the total resources of the life-substance in the universe is one of the most characteristic and significant in the whole history of mankind.'[6]

The establishment of settled communities, the emergence of an agricultural civilization in the great river valleys, the evolution of social hierarchies, all demanded that sacrificial ritual, while retaining in many instances the familiar pattern of blood sacrifice, should be diversified and should recognise the priority that must be given to the cultivation of the soil and the growth of the crops. The victim might take a variety of forms, but the vegetation offering emerges, therefore, at an early stage as something that is of great antiquity and second only in importance to the blood sacrifice.

Seasonal rituals were established which corresponded with the rhythms of the world of nature, the cycle of the earth. The fertility of the land – like the fertility of man and beast – was essential to survival. The supply of food must be guaranteed. There is an awareness here of the female principle in the processes of fertility and generation, but there is no uniform pattern of behaviour and there seems to be no single goal to be pursued. Agrarian sacrifices, vegetation offerings, might take a variety of forms and serve a variety of purposes. It was through the offering of the first-fruits that the whole flock or the whole harvest would be consecrated. It was through the offering of the oblationary sacrifice that developed societies maintained and renewed their internal cohesion and wellbeing as every level made its appropriate offering in kind. Vegetation offerings were related to the seasons of the year, to the cycle of nature, to the obligations of society.

It is necessary also to acknowledge the significance of human sacrifice. This phenomenon was to be found most frequently in the more developed agricultural societies. It might well have been concerned to secure the fertility of the land in the first instance; but there were undoubtedly other connotations, including the maintenance or the restoration of right relations between man and man or man and the supernatural order. The primary aims of the worshippers were to protect the life of the community, to avert danger and to renew the mainsprings of life-giving energy. The life was in the blood and there was judged to be a special potency in human blood. It followed inevitably that in some societies the rituals that were associated with the killing of sacral kings were judged to be the most efficacious. It is in the early practices of offering the life of an individual for the sake of the community – and the sacrifice of animals as substitute or surrogate victims for man must be included here – that the earliest ideas of substitution and propitiation can be discerned.

Ideas of substitution, identification and participation counted for much in some primitive rites. They provide an insight into what is meant by the power, the creative energy, of sacrifice. Evans-Pritchard's studies of the Nuer, a cattle-herding people who lived in the swamps and the savannahs of the southern Sudan, provide us with a contemporary illustration of the force of these concepts.[7] His account of what the sacrifice actually means for the people is dramatic in its simplicity. 'When Nuer give their cattle in sacrifice they are very much, and in a very intimate way, giving part of themselves. What they surrender are living creatures, gifts more expressive of the self and with a closer resemblance to it than inanimate things, and these living creatures are the most precious of their possessions, so much so that they can be said to participate in them to the point of identification'.[8] Evans-Pritchard acknowledges the variations in the ritual and the different shades of meaning that are carried by their sacrifices, but he concludes that 'if we have to sum up the meaning of Nuer sacrifice in a single word or idea, I would say that it is a substitution, *vita pro vita*'.[9]

It is in exactly this sense that G. Van Der Leeuw interprets the deeper meaning of the gift offered in sacrifice. He takes the Latin word *dare* and he emphasises that it means 'to place oneself in relation to, and then to participate in, a second person by means of an object, which however is not actually an object at all, but a part of one's own self'.[10] The giver and the receiver both participate in the gift. Van Der Leeuw insists that the giver and the receiver both participate, therefore, in each other. The gift has power. It is a binding force.[11]

Sacrificial rites served many purposes but they possessed one common characteristic. They were believed to work. Hubert and Mauss may well have been anticipating later theories when they wrote of the religious energy set free by sacrifices,[12] but J. H. M. Beattie concludes that 'almost always sacrifice is seen as being, mostly, about *power*, or *powers*'.[13] The power of the sacrifice was a sensitive and complex force. It was a power that could make for life or death. Hubert and Mauss, writing with special reference to the Vedic Hindu sacrifice of animals but drawing upon a

wider experience of sacrificial ritual, emphasised the importance that was attached to a meticulous attention to every
detail of the rite. The forces at work could so easily turn
against the person who offers the sacrifice and the person or
cause for which the sacrifice is offered. The power of the
sacrifice is determined not merely by external observance but
by interior attitudes. The victim is 'a focus of energy'.[14] The
successful deployment of that energy requires not only an
exact obedience to the procedures of the ritual but a con-
stancy of mind and purpose in the offering of the sacrifice
and an unshakeable confidence in the power of the rites. The
power of the sacrifice lies in the rite and in the gift. A sacrifice
was a costly thing. In the giving up, in the handing over,
above all in the shedding of blood, power was released –
enabling, integrating, life-giving power. The heart of these
ancient rites – the true meaning of sacrifice – is to be found
in their power.

# Chapter 9

# Sacrifice in the Old Testament

Sacrifice – the concept and the institution – is deeply rooted in the Old Testament. The classes of sacrifice are numerous. The vocabulary is extensive. The Old Testament does not provide any rationale for sacrifice. It is taken for granted as a divine ordinance. The stories of the patriarchs suggest that the cultus in its various forms has a long history. All the circumstances of daily life might be occasions for offering sacrifices, although the associations – especially in earlier centuries – are those of an agricultural society. The sacrifices had their origin in similar rites among neighbouring peoples but their meaning was adapted and transformed because of the theological interpretation that later Israel placed upon the nation's story.

Inferences concerning sacrificial worship will often be tentative. Much of the Old Testament material regarding sacrifice probably reached its present form around 500 BC, but there had previously been a long period of oral and literary transmission. The Old Testament documents are complex and it is necessary to recognise the developments that occurred within the sacrificial system over many centuries. Old Testament sacrifice can only be interpreted in the light of the covenant relationship that God had established with his people. Its significance was ultimately to be found in the conviction that God is the Lord of history, that He had chosen Israel to be His people, that obedience to His law is life and not death.

The spontaneous character of many sacrifices which marked the earlier period of Old Testament history gave way from the seventh century B.C. to a comprehensive system of

71

cultic regulations, culminating in Josiah's reforms and the centralization of worship in 621. There is ample evidence of the existence of a popular cultus – syncretistic and irregular – which takes a variety of forms, but it is difficult to get behind the documents and the orthodoxy of a later period. Three principal types of sacrifice came to dominate Jewish practice – the communion sacrifice or peace offering, the whole-burnt offering, and the sin or guilt offering.

The communion sacrifice embraced the thank offering, the votive offering and the freewill offering. Its primary purpose appears to have been the renewal or restoration of the relationship between the worshipper and Yahweh. It would often take the form of a personal or family sacrifice. The note of celebration was probably most dominant. It was essentially a meal, an act of thanksgiving and of communion with God. Similar ideas were to be found in the meal offering, the drink offering, the memorial offering and the shewbread. Many of these go back to very early times. All contained the notion of making a gift to God, but also perhaps of nourishing God.

The most regular and the most important sacrifice was the whole-burnt offering. Although it might be offered as a private sacrifice, it was normally used as a public sacrifice. The origins of the whole-burnt sacrifice are uncertain, but the common notion of the sacrifice as a gift is most obviously present in this offering. The evidence suggests that the peace offering and the whole-burnt offering were common in Israel before the Babylonian exile. The whole-burnt offering was the sacrifice that was given entirely to God. It represented in its ideal form the absolute commitment of His people.

It was only after the exile and in the light of the teaching of the great prophets of the eighth and seventh centuries B.C. that the sin and guilt offerings became so prominent. They were offered for sins committed in ignorance. The difference between the sin offering and the guilt offering is not entirely clear. The sin offering was the sacrifice that was offered to make atonement for offences against God's holiness. The guilt offering was concerned to make expiation for dues withheld from God and from man. Sin and guilt offerings reflect the prophetic call for righteousness. They have a closer relation to sin and expiation than either the communion sacrifice or the whole-burnt offering.

The relationship between sacrifice and morality was a primary prophetic theme. Jeremiah alone amongst the prophets was willing to go so far as to make obedience to the moral requirements of God a substitute for the cultus, but the abuses of the sacrificial system were denounced by the pre-exilic prophets. The righteousness of God demanded a holy people. The faith of Judaism with its distinctive emphasis upon the sovereignty and righteousness of God transformed the Hebrew understanding of sacrifice.

There is no one theory that can explain the sacrificial system of the Old Testament. The rites do not permit simple explanations. One element might be dominant in one type of sacrifice, but other elements might also be present. Some elements in the tradition retained their significance and provided threads of continuity, but sacrifices meant different things to different groups within the community at different times. All sacrifices were concerned with restoring or maintaining or renewing fellowship with God.

It is this understanding of sacrifice which is drawn out by F. C. N. Hicks in designating the six stages that would normally be present in the rites – first, the worshipper draws near with his offering; secondly, he lays his hands on the victim's head as an act of identification; thirdly, he kills the victim; fourthly, the priest presents the blood to God by pouring it upon, or dashing it against, the altar; fifthly, the flesh, or a part of it, is burnt and is thus transformed so that it might ascend to God; and, finally, a portion of the offering is eaten by priest and worshipper, except in the case of the whole-burnt offering, while the flesh of the sin offering and the guilt offering is reserved for the priest except when atonement is made for his own sins.[1]

This is a composite, an idealised, picture. The sacrifice is to be found in the whole activity of the rite. It is not located in a single part. The representative character of the sacrifice is made abundantly plain. The worshipper identifies with his offering and, while it is presented to God, he participates in it himself. And, of course, the fundamental importance of blood is enshrined in this ritual – 'For the life of the flesh is in the blood; and I have given it for you upon the altar to make atonement for your souls; for it is the blood that makes atonement, by reason of the life'.[2] The life is in the blood, and blood is offered so that life might be renewed and restored. Blood was important in all types of sacrifice, but it took on a special significance in the case of sin or guilt offerings. Sacrifices were not all related to the expiation of sin and, where they were, the law required confession, penitence and reparation. Only, then, could sacrifice lead from death to life. Sacrifice was potent. It was able to bring things about. It could effect change. The sacrifices of the Old Testament – including the blood sacrifices – can only be understood within the context of the covenant relationship between a righteous God and His people.

The Babylonian exile formed a very sharp line of demarcation in the understanding and practice of sacrifice in ancient Israel. The great annual festivals of Judaism were originally derived from the life of an agricultural people. In the reforms of the sacrificial system that followed upon the exile and in the centralization of worship at the temple in Jerusalem, the festivals became associated far more with significant events in Israel's history.

Old practices were invested with new meaning. The Day of Atonement was a feast not a fast. It was the most important day of the year. Certain aspects of its ritual – especially that part of it which related to the scapegoat – went back to the earliest times in the history of the people. It was an occasion when sacrifices would be offered for the High Priest, for the priests and for the people. It was essentially a corporate act of atonement for a nation which had found its vocation and identity in its covenant relationship with a righteous God. The Feasts of Passover and Unleavened Bread commemorated the Exodus. The Feast of Tabernacles recalled the wanderings in the wilderness. The Feast of Weeks or Pentecost celebrated the giving of the law on Sinai. All these rites had their origins in earlier cultures. It has been suggested that Passover was originally a lambing festival, that Unleavened Bread was held at the beginning of the barley harvest, that Tabernacles marked the gathering in of the fruit harvest. It may be that earlier sacrificial rituals are preserved in these observances.

It is not difficult in these circumstances to see how rites, originally associated with the rhythms of the life of an agricultural society and essentially joyful in character, might become solemn anniversaries in the remembrance of the saving events of a nation's history. And so the Passover ritual provided an interpretation of the Exodus deliverance, and the telling of the story had its special place in the performance of the rite. The prophetic call to repentance and to righteousness prepared the way for the sin and guilt offerings and for the new dimensions in the ritual which, while they retained the note of festival and of corporate activity, introduced an element of historical selfconsciousness and of a celebration of new life through the shedding of blood as an act of expiation and atonement.

Christian theology interprets Jewish sacrificial rites as activities that find their full meaning only in the life, death and resurrection of Jesus Christ. They are, therefore, for Christian theology preparatory rites of great symbolism. They point beyond themselves to the new covenant relationship that God will establish with His people. Nothing can diminish, however, the meaning that these early rites carried for their own people and their own time. They addressed the fundamental human dilemma – the search for wholeness, the awareness of God, the experience of estrangement, the reality of evil, man's personal and corporate responsibility, the mystery of atonement.

It is within the continuing life of the nation that the sacrificial system evolved, expressing the mind and spirit of the people. Its primary concerns were relationships between God and man, and between man and man. The Old Testament story – the election of a people, the deliverance out of slavery in Egypt, the covenant relationship, the ethical demands of a holy God – was re-enacted in sacrifice. The Old Testament themes of redemption and judgement and righteousness were expressed in sacrifice. The connection between sacrifice and sin was strong in Jewish thought, but it would be a travesty of Jewish theology to suggest that the inner spirit was a matter of secondary concern or that the sacrifice effected the atonement. The severest condemnation of the prophets was reserved for those who acted as though the sacrifice was sufficient in itself to remove the guilt of sin. The ritual required the validation that could only be provided by the disposition of the heart and which thus secured the power of the sacrifice.[3]

The ancient conviction that sacrifice is essentially about the release of power, of life-giving energy, takes on a new meaning. The sacrifice does not accomplish the atonement. Atonement involves both the removal of sin and the reconciliation of the sinner. The cultic regulations enabled those who stood within the covenant to offer sacrifice as an expiation for sin, but atonement was God's activity. It was His work of grace. The sacrificial system provided the means whereby man could draw near to God, and God could draw near to man in power.

There is one additional element in the Old Testament which demands attention. The Suffering Servant passages of Deutero-Isaiah[4] speak of one who will inaugurate God's kingdom of righteousness and whose sacrifice of obedience, which will entail rejection and grievous suffering, will be the effective sign of his mission. There is contained in these passages the notion of a substitutionary death. The Servant is to be an offering for sin and it is by virtue of his righteousness that many shall be accounted righteous. Here is something that goes beyond the prescribed rituals of the priestly code. It is a type of sacrifice which cannot be brought within the bounds of the peace offering, the whole-burnt offering, or the sin offering. It might be argued that there is a sense in which the Suffering Servant takes to Himself all these types, but this is to anticipate the judgement of Christian faith which interprets these passages in the light of its experience of redemption through the cross of Christ. It is doubtful if Judaism ever saw any connection between the Servant and the Messiah. H. H. Rowley concludes that the Servant is probably 'in part the personification of the mission of Israel, and in part the delineation of one who should embody its mission in himself'.[5]

The sacrifices of the Old Testament go beyond the primitive rites, expressing something of the personal and communal act of celebration that was contained within the ancient ceremonies, linking a developed ritual with the story of a people, and participating through the mature faith of the covenant relationship in the life of God. The Suffering Servant – set within the total context of biblical revelation – points forward to the One who will display the fullness of the meaning and the power of sacrifice.

*Chapter 10*

# The Meaning of Sacrifice

The experience of Judaism continues to be a vital resource for Christian theology. The church interpreted and developed in its early years, in the light of its experience, the sacrificial thought and practices of Israel and of the Mediterranean world in which it emerged and evolved. The destruction of the temple at Jerusalem in AD 70 led to the abandonment of the Jewish sacrificial system, but the Old Testament continues to connect us with a world that has almost entirely disappeared and to remind us of the central place that was assigned to sacrifice by so many primitive cultures and early civilizations in different parts of the world.

Ancient rites were concerned with identity and meaning, but they belong to another world, and their relevance to us today is not immediately apparent. Anthropological studies will only assist our purpose if they can demonstrate that the insights of primitive man make connections – albeit unwittingly – with something that is fundamental to life and, therefore, of abiding significance. It is relatively easy to make observations on the basis of these studies about the relationship of sacrifice to the needs of man and of community life. But general observations beg far larger questions that continue to surround the meaning of sacrifice. What are the fundamental truths that are expressed by sacrificial rites? Was primitive man so much more fully in touch with the rhythms of his world that he possessed some intuitive awareness of how life works? Is it possible to discern in all these things some recognition of a basic principle – the element of sacrifice – which demands to be acknowledged as one of the primary ingredients in the structures and relationships of life?

78

Any discussion of the true meaning of sacrifice is confused and obscured by the way in which the word has been used and the associations it has assumed in people's minds. The symbolism of sacrifice is too evocative to be ignored and, therefore, too readily available to be distorted and abused for partisan purposes. The word has taken to itself – and not least of all in times of war – a good deal of public rhetoric, popular sentiment and personal piety. The notion that sacrifice is essentially a voluntary act of self-destruction for the good of some great cause contains an element of truth, but it fails to do justice to the depth of meaning, the richness and the power that the word possesses. And unless the concept of sacrifice can be explored within a theological framework – that is to say, within all that theology understands about the mystery of God – it will be impossible to penetrate its meaning. Ancient sacrificial rites have long since been abandoned or transmuted and transformed; but men and women retain the capacity to recognise the authority and the power of sacrificial lives. The experience of sacrifice continues to touch depths within our common life, providing moments of life through death to which a bewildered and tormented race turns in hope.

It is helpful to turn in the first instance to the meaning of sacrifice. The popular use of the word fails to convey the religious sense, the note of celebration, the communal activity, the joyfulness that were features of so many ancient rites. The emphasis falls now on the destruction or the surrender or the loss of someone or something that is valued, on the act of abandonment, of laying down, of giving up. These connotations were undoubtedly present in many sacrificial rituals, but they were present in a positive and not a negative sense. The object that was given in sacrifice had power because the giver and the receiver both participated in the gift. It is necessary to distinguish between the contemporary use of the word and its true meaning. 'The word sacrifice in our language means always losing something, being deprived of something. But in Latin, in Greek, in Hebrew, in Slavonic, in all the ancient languages, sacrifice comes from sacred – it means to make something sacred, make something holy and not to lose it. Indeed, when you bring a life to God or a gift to God, it becomes His, it is no longer yours in the greedy and possessive sense of the word. But it becomes holy with the holiness of God'.[1] Christian hope speaks of the wholeness, the holiness, the at-one-ment that God wills for His creation. The love which is grounded in God involves the giver and the receiver in sacrifice.

Christian hope speaks of the conviction that the creation will find its fulfilment, its completeness, in God. It is sacrifice that makes the connection between the holiness of God, our search for wholeness, and the hope that God will be all in all. God manages His creation and His redemption in such a way that He puts Himself at risk. Creative and redemptive love involves sacrifice. To be made whole, to become holy with the holiness of God, presupposes the sacrifice in which the giver and the receiver – God and man, man and God – both participate in the gift. The origin of the word gives us the all-important insight into the meaning of sacrifice.

Christian theology is able to take up our search for wholeness and set it within a wider frame of reference because it cannot ultimately be separated from the holiness of God and the at-one-ment that He wills for His creation. Holistic models of God, holistic theories of atonement, require symbols. Sacrificial ritual takes us back in the second place to what has already been said about the power of symbols to make whole that which is disconnected or fragmented. The gift theory and the communion theory of sacrifice both speak of man's desire to secure his place within his world, to belong, to be at one with the vital forces of life. The offering that was made to a deity took on a range and depth of meaning. It represented man. It gathered to itself the joys, the fears, the hopes, the guilts of the people. The ancient rites brought into play the universal symbols of food and water, fire and blood. The meaning of sacrifice cannot be separated from the power of symbols.

But a symbol has power because it participates in the reality that it represents. The animal that is offered in sacrifice becomes a symbol of his people's story, their aspirations and their needs. But a symbol is an active principle. It has power.

There is a dynamic which is present and which cannot be ignored. It might almost be compared with the biblical experience of the prophet who speaks the word which brings the events to pass. Past, present and future are brought together as experience and interpretation interact upon each other. A symbol continues to speak of the mystery of things. It points beyond itself. It gives coherence and meaning to our world. It is able to bind together, to make whole.

Sacrifice and symbol belong together and cannot be eliminated. The desire for sacrifice, the need for symbols, will find expression in one way or another. But if the reality of which sacrifice and symbol speak is the life of God, the way things are, or ought to be, the truth of our condition, questions have to be asked about the danger that is being done if sacrifice and symbol are removed from the framework of our lives. Is this the vacuum that has been occupied by those who use the language of sacrifice to serve their own ends? Is this the appalling emptiness in which symbols of fanaticism and hatred and deep division find a place? It is an impoverished society that has lost all awareness of the power of symbols. A discovery of the signs of the mystery of atonement will involve a rediscovery of the symbols by which we live. The symbol system of the Christian religion is inseparable from sacrifice.

There is a third consideration which is fundamental to any holistic theory of atonement. Our knowledge of ancient sacrificial rites puts before us the recurring *motif* of life and death and life. The sacrificial process of passing from life through death to life was believed to be the means whereby relationships were established with the supernatural order. The primitive conviction – attested in the Old Testament – that the life is in the blood has long since been abandoned, but the potency of blood sacrifice as a means of renewing the vitality of a community has not been entirely lost. Blood has been intimately associated in men's minds with the symbolism of sacrifice. Here is something that defies all rational explanation. The sacrifice of blood – for good or for ill – still retains something of its ancient power. Dillistone suggests that blood has increased its power as a symbol in the contemporary world. He quotes Indira Gandhi as saying shortly before her assassination that, 'Unless the blood circulates, the body dies'.[2] We are brought very close here to all that we mean by the element of sacrifice within the dynamics of life. The instances that might be cited are too numerous. They constitute the infinite number of unseen deaths in which the part, by virtue of its own destruction, renews the life of the whole.

Blood is the symbol of life and death. It is important only because it speaks of the pattern of life and death and life. So common is this pattern that it must be regarded as one of the primary ingredients in the structures and relationships of our world. Dillistone asks us to face the theological consequences and questions that are raised by this sign of the pattern of things. 'So enduring and so universal does this pattern seem to be, that it becomes altogether natural to imagine that this is in fact the essential pattern of the life of God Himself'.[3] And so the questions are pressed: 'Does death lead forward to the renewal of life?'[4]; 'How can (man) hope to be reintegrated into the original, the creative, the constitutive pattern of all existence?';[5] and if it is true that 'the ultimate principle of existence . . . is *through-death-to-life* . . . is it possible to conceive such an activity taking place within the being of God Himself?'.[6]

The questions suggest a place for sacrifice within the general scheme of things which is far larger than anything that has yet been envisaged. There is, however, one final point of which note must be taken. The ancient sacrificial rites were essentially about power. Sacrifice was 'the centre of a dynamic process in which the divine and human came into contact'.[7] It was there at the heart of this process that power was released.

There is something here that is entirely consistent with the meaning of sacrifice which is the power to make holy, with the meaning of symbols which is the power to make whole, with the meaning of this recurring pattern which is the power to lead from life through death to life. Is sacrifice the life-giving breath of God? Is this the power that lies buried deep within the patterns of interdependence and interaction, the elements of necessity and chance? Is this the principle of life that makes for new life? Man continues to look upon himself with the eyes of a stranger. The experience of alienation remains. 'Man is estranged from himself and from God until he can sacrifice every part of his self for the sake of a larger harmony. He must become Whole, that is, Holy'.[8] But atonement is the work of God. Sacrifice speaks of God's power to make holy, to make whole.

# PART IV

# THE WORK OF CHRIST

## Chapter 11

# The Work of Christ

The questions that have been asked concerning the place of sacrifice within the life of God lead inevitably in Christian theology to an exposition of the work of Christ. The early proclamation that God was in Christ reconciling the world to Himself[1] raises immediately the impossibility of separating the event from the interpretation. The event encompasses the whole life of Jesus. The interpretation is the meaning that was attached to these events by the early church in the light of the experience of death and resurrection. The event is presented as the activity of God but the interpretation is the judgement of faith and it is part of that judgement to portray the event as God's activity.

The preaching of the Christian gospel took on from the beginning the familiar biblical form of narrative[2]. The telling of the story is an appropriate means of communication for an historical religion. It is in the telling of the story that the meaning of the man is to be found. Biblical narrative always carries its own interpretation. The event in which faith is grounded lies in the past; the meaning is to be drawn out in the present and the future.

The Christian story, which is the basis of Christian faith and hope, requires a response that is critical and imaginative, rational and intuitive. There is a great deal of data to be interpreted: the life and work of Jesus as they are recorded in the gospels; the fact of His death and the experience of His resurrection; the evidence of the early church – the emergence of Christianity, its rapid expansion during the apostolic age, its perception of itself as the Body of Christ; the distinctive forms of Christian experience and expression – the gift of the Spirit, baptism and eucharist; the early development of a high Christology; the experience of Christian people down the centuries. These are not disparate elements. They inform and question and confirm each other. They constitute a *corpus* of experience that demands constant scrutiny.

The evidence of scripture is irreplaceable but it does not stand alone. The reconstruction of the life of Jesus is bound to be tentative and uncertain, and it will be constantly open to re-interpretation. The truth of the Christian story can only be demonstrated if it is seen to be true both to itself and to our knowledge of the world and our experience as human beings. It is the continuing evidence that is afforded by the experience of Jesus that brings the church back to the task of reconstruction. It is as though there can be discerned in the life and death and resurrection of Jesus a pattern which corresponds with a wider experience of the world.

Christian hope unites the past and the future in the person and the work of Jesus. The eschatological character of the early Christian proclamation comes out of the belief that the Jewish scriptures find their fulfilment in Jesus. He is the prophet who has been raised up by God[3], the servant who has been glorified by the God of Abraham, Isaac and Jacob.[4] God has acted decisively in Jesus to inaugurate a new covenant relationship, a new age of righteousness.[5] God has confirmed His work by the pouring out of the Holy Spirit.[6]

It was the ferment of ideas and aspirations in contemporary Judaism that shaped the direction in which Christian thought developed. The most familiar titles applied to Jesus had their origins in the expectations of Jewish eschatology.[7] It is necessary to look to Jewish sources to find some of the important building-blocks used by the early church in the development of its Christology – pre-existence, mediation at creation, incarnation.[8] The concept of incarnation provided a way of interpreting messiahship in the light of the death and resurrection of Jesus, but the priority for the early church lay not with incarnation but messiahship.[9]

All statements concerning the person of Jesus are partial and incomplete. The composite language of New Testament Christology brings together historical statements, theological affirmations, and metaphysical propositions. The relatively early designation of Jesus as the One in whom all the fullness of God was pleased to dwell[10] cannot be accounted for unless it is assumed that a Christology was to be found in the earliest traditions and was implicit, even, in some of the sayings of Jesus that have been preserved in the gospels.[11]

A two-nature Christology does not easily commend itself to the contemporary mind. It belongs to a metaphaphysical framework within which it is not customary to work. It suggests a breach in the pattern of God's relationship with the world which is out of character with all that is known about His activity. The unique status that it assigns to Jesus makes Him less credible, less compelling, for some. It leaves so many unanswered and unanswerable questions. It is against the background of these problems that one notable alternative – a Spirit Christology – has been proposed.[12] Such a Christology makes it possible to say that Jesus is authentically human, capable of responding freely to God, and of being the instrument of mediation between God and man. His distinguishing mark is the completeness of His obedience to God's calling. There is, therefore, a union of God with man in Jesus, which enables us to encounter God, but in that union 'God is truly God and man is authentically man.'[13]

This re-presentation of Christology shifts the emphasis from the activity of God to the obedience of man. It is the integrity of Jesus' obedience that compels. He is the one who shows what it means to go the whole way, and in so doing He becomes the One who shows us the mystery of God. It is, then, possible to go on from the person of Jesus to the nature of God's relations with man, and to speak of 'a continuous *kenosis* of God as Spirit', a relationship of interaction in which man is free to respond or to reject, to claim if he so chooses the freedom of responsible sonship.[14] There is much here that is consistent with all that must be affirmed concerning God's self-revelation; but a Spirit Christology, although it retains the echoes of a traditional Christology, scarcely does justice to the unique character of God's initiative in Jesus.

A traditional incarnational two-nature Christology retains

the advantage that it brings together in the most economical form all that must be said about God, His relationship to man, His redemption. To question a Spirit Christology is not to deny that in the incarnate life of Christ there is to be found the pattern of self-limitation, self-emptying and active participation that are the distinctive marks of God in His relation to man. Nor is it to deny that Jesus possessed the same capacity for self-awareness, freedom and power that are the corresponding marks of man in his relation to God. The incarnation speaks of God's absolute and irrevocable self-giving. It is an activity within God. 'The whole work of God lives and moves in this one Person. He who says God in the sense of Holy Scripture will necessarily have to say Jesus Christ over and over again.'[15]

There is a totality about the biblical revelation. And so it is that for Barth there is implicit in the election of Israel the incarnation of the Son because 'God has from the very first offered, surrendered and sacrificed no less than something of Himself . . . so that from the very first the existence of Israel includes in itself the existence of the Son of God on earth'.[16] The biblical story leads, therefore, through the incarnation to an understanding of God which identifies Him as a partner in our story which is also His story. It is in this sense that world history and salvation history are brought together and become one.[17] Through the incarnation, God has not merely taken to Himself the life of our humanity by entering our world, He has chosen to represent the whole of our humanity in the person of His Son.

The work of Christ incorporates the eschatological hope that He will conclude all things in His own person. The consequences of this work are inseparable from the Christian hope. There is a parallel between Israel's experience of God and the church's experience of Jesus. It was through God's activity in the Exodus and all the events of their history that the Israelites discovered their identity as the people of God. 'When Israel was a child I loved him, and out of Egypt I called my son'.[18] It was through God's activity in Jesus and the whole experience of redemption that the early church came to believe that 'in these last days (God) has spoken to us by a Son',[19] and that through incorporation in Him we might become the sons of God. The purpose of the incarnation is the mystery of our atonement. It is participation in God. 'God became what we are so that He might make us what He is.'[20]

The truth about Jesus is ultimately a question of personal encounter; but the four propositions that provide the framework for a holistic theory of atonement must be tested by all that the church desires to say about Jesus. If it is true that any theory of atonement must proceed from our understanding of who God is and what God does, then its capacity to be illuminated by and to illuminate both Trinitarian faith and incarnational Christology becomes all-important. The four propositions of a holistic theory of atonement have been impressed upon us by an attempt to understand the world in which we live. But it is necessary to bring within their compass all that the church must say about the nature and the work of Christ. This is not to suggest that they can be some literary device for accommodating the life and death and resurrection of Jesus. They cannot be allowed to stand unchallenged unless they provide an intelligible way of speaking about the work of Christ.

First, the patterns of interdependence and interaction illuminate a traditional Christology in a variety of ways. If it is true that in Jesus all the fullness of God was pleased to dwell,[21] then all that is understood by God and man are brought together in a new relationship of interdependence. The exploration of God and man can no longer be separated from each other. It is because of Christology that Rahner insists that henceforth theology and anthropology belong together.[22]

Jesus is the One who holds all things together.[23] He is the pre-eminent symbol of the Christian religion, embodying 'the mystery behind and above and within all that exists'.[24] God's relationship with His people finds its full expression in Jesus. Creation, redemption and sanctification are brought together in this One person as one process. God's purposes are lived out in Him.

But Jesus is also 'the central symbol, potentially uniting the whole of humanity to God Himself'.[25] If it is true that we are all bound up in one another as members of the human race, that all men are ultimately one because all life is held in God, then it is possible to suggest that in Jesus we encounter the one truly representative man. But such an assertion must be explored within the framework of this first proposition. Its meaning must include the belief that the material world, all human history, are brought together in Jesus. 'Jesus is true man; He is truly a part of the earth, truly a moment in the biological evolution of this world, a moment of human history, for He is born of a woman'.[26] The incarnation provides, therefore, a way of understanding the human drama as an integrated phenomenon.

The claim that Jesus is in some sense the representative man is now given a wider definition. He represents our humanity; but the whole of our humanity, including man's relationship with the created order, is now contained within Jesus and, therefore, within God. But this representative and inclusive character can only be sustained on the basis of an incarnational Christology. By contrast with every man's distinction from his neighbour, Jesus makes explicit the fundamental reality that life is constantly upheld by God because in Jesus God comes into His world and becomes one with His creation and calls us to become one with Him in Christ.

Secondly, a plain reading of the gospel narrative suggests that necessity and chance, spontaneity and choice, competition and conflict were notable features both of Jesus' self-awareness and of his public ministry. The temptations in the wilderness,[27] the teaching concerning the kingdom,[28] the recognition by the evil spirits,[29] the determination to destroy Him[30] all have their place; but it is in its presentation of the passion that the gospel tradition illuminates most clearly the interplay between necessity and chance.

The element of necessity is grounded in the suffering love of God. The element of chance is contained in the freedom God gives to His creation. The Son of Man goes as it is written of Him[31] but Jesus is portrayed as an active participant. 'When the days drew near for Him to be received up, He set His face to go to Jerusalem'.[32] Jesus is the Lamb slain from before the foundation of the world; but this external necessity became 'an act of sovereign creative power'.[33] Jesus responds in faith. The prayer in Gethsemane conveys it all: 'My Father, if it be possible, let this cup pass from me; nevertheless, not as I will, but as thou wilt'.[34]

The tension between what God wills and what man permits is basic to the way in which God chooses to work. It is 'divine prevenience *and* human response' that are brought together so completely in the story of Jesus.[35] Man stands before God in his self-awareness, his freedom and his power. Christology demands that we take full account of 'the whole reality of man in his unity and free responsibility'.[36] God's purposes require our glad co-operation.

Thirdly, it is in the cross that the element of sacrifice is to be found. It is in the life and death and resurrection of Jesus that Christian faith distinguishes the *motif* of life and death and life. It is inconceivable that Jesus should not have died. He entered the human predicament so fully that He shared its impotence and mortality. Evil could not remain outside God's dealings with the world. The challenge that Jesus represented exposed the evil and drew it into Himself. A traditional Christology which identifies Jesus as the representative man is able to say that, 'He gathers into His humanity the whole of humanity, every person who ever was or ever will be'.[37] It is this conviction that underlies Paul's argument that one has died for all and, therefore, all have died.[38] Jesus does not die 'only *for* mankind but *as* mankind'.[39] But this proposition is concerned with life and death *and life*. 'Unless a grain of wheat falls into the earth and dies, it remains alone; but if it dies, it bears much fruit'.[40]

Birth and death belong together. John Donne captures this truth in his *Sermon On Christmas Day*. 'The whole life of Christ was a continual Passion. . . . His birth and death were but one continual act, and His Christmas Day and His Good Friday are but the evening and morning of one and the same day'.[41] Christian obedience requires the Christian disciple to share in the pattern of death and resurrection, laying aside the old nature and putting on the new nature which is being renewed in knowledge after the image of its creator.[42]

Fourthly, there is the promise of new life. If God is the supreme symbol of man's search for wholeness, it is Jesus who is the God-given symbol of reconciliation, the author of new life. The covenant relationship spoke of God's will for His people. The eschatological hope presupposed the coming of God's kingly rule, the establishment of a new order of righteousness. The preaching of the early church suggests that the resurrection of Jesus was seen as both a fulfilment of the covenant relationship and a sign that the last days had arrived. The resurrection of Jesus comes within any consideration of this fourth proposition. The resurrection is not merely an act of divine intervention and vindication. It is a sign of the purposes of God. The meaning of Jesus is to be found in the eschatological hope of the early church. 'To speak of the resurrection of the dead was to speak of the life of the Age to come'.[43]

The life of the age to come has two initiating marks – the experience of resurrection and the experience of the Spirit. Both experiences speak of the purposes and the power of God. The resurrection of Jesus – the first fruits of those who have fallen asleep[44] – is the sign of a new order of being. Its consequences are universal. Every rule and every authority and power – including death – must be destroyed.[45] The whole cosmic order is to be transformed so that God may be all in all.[46] And the Spirit is the guarantee of God's purposes. It is the law of the Spirit of life in Christ Jesus that sets us free from the law of sin and death.[47] The work of Christ and the work of the Spirit cannot be separated – 'you were washed, you were sanctified, you were justified in the name of the Lord Jesus Christ and in the Spirit of our God'.[48] And the promise of new life is found in the conviction that all who are led by the Spirit of God are sons of God.[49]

It is in association with Christ that man is to be brought into a new order of being. 'Among the sons of men the Lord Jesus only has appeared, in whom all have been crucified, all are dead and buried, all again have been raised'.[50] It is another consequence of the concept of Jesus as the representative man that He shows us 'man as he is called to be. . . . Man becomes truly human only when he is united with God infinitely, deeply, inseparably, so that the fullness of Godhead abides in the flesh'.[51] The argument returns again to the final hope of participation in the life of God. This is the new covenant that God establishes with His people. 'What Christ is, all others are potentially involved in becoming'.[52] It is the work of Christ to give the wholeness, the atonement, that we seek.

*Chapter 12*

# The Kingdom of God

It was through His proclamation of the kingdom of God that Jesus issued His invitation to enter into life. His task was to bear witness to the truth.[1] His purpose was to do the Father's will.[2] And there was an element of compulsion as Jesus went about His work, drawing men and women towards the kingdom, attempting to bring them within the compass of God's sovereign power. The basis of His prophetic call was the conviction, rooted in the eschatological hopes of His time, that God was present in a new and decisive way in the story of His people. Jewish eschatology brought together the kingdom of God and the fatherhood of God. God would vindicate His people. He would come to them in righteousness and judgement. He would dwell with them and care for them.

The Messianic hope persisted in the century before the birth of Jesus and the gospels provide ample evidence of the strength of that hope in the first half of the first century A.D. The most notable titles by which Jesus is known – Messiah, Son of Man, Son of God, Lord, Logos – are all to be found in non-Christian writings before their adoption by the early church. Their application to Jesus meant that they were inevitably given a new meaning.[3] These titles carry a range of meanings and can be interpreted in a variety of ways. The most familiar title by which Jesus is known in the gospels – Son of Man – has scarcely any place in other early Christian literature,[4] but it seems to be inseparable from all the ideas that surrounded Jesus' message concerning the establishment of the kingdom of God.[5]

The relationship between the kingdom of God and the fatherhood of God is lived out first in Jesus' own experience.

He is the One on whom the Father has set His seal.[6] He is the One to whom all things have been delivered by the Father.[7] The relationship of a father and a son would have had certain connotations within Judaism. The son is frequently referred to as being in the loins of his father. It was the father who gave his name and, therefore, his identity to the son. It was through the son that the life and work of the father might be continued.

The relationship with the Father was the ground of His being. The intimacy of the relationship is captured by the way in which Jesus addressed God as *abba*. An examination of the prayer literature of ancient Judaism led Joachim Jeremias to conclude that Jesus' use of this intimate form of address was without precedent; but it was the way in which Jesus always spoke to the Father with one exception: the cry from the cross, 'My God, my God, why hast thou forsaken me?'[8] Jesus' unique sense that 'the Father is in me and I am in the Father'[9] was the basis of His whole ministry.

The proclamation of the kingdom is the central theme of the ministry of Jesus. It is pursued with great urgency. The explanation of Jesus' position seems to be His conviction that His ministry is being lived and acted out at a decisive moment. The proclamation cannot be divorced from His own injunction to go the whole way or to enter into life.[10] It was out of the depths of His relationship with the Father that Jesus was able to 'speak of what we know, and bear witness to what we have seen'.[11] The signs of the kingdom were to be the means by which His obedience and His authority might be recognised and His Father glorified. Jesus brought together in His own person so many Old Testament themes. It was, however, His obedience to the call to be *my son* which made it possible to live out and speak of all the others – the covenant relationship, judgement and mercy, the Suffering Servant, the kingdom of God. Jesus knew what it meant to live out God's purpose in His own life: 'He who loves father or mother more than me is not worthy of me; and he who does not take his cross and follow me is not of me. He who finds his life will lose it, and he who loses his life for my sake will find it'.[12]

These words convey the uncompromising demand that
Jesus made of Himself and of those to whom He brought the
good news. His proclamation of the good news was a prophetic word. It contained judgement and promise. He was a
teacher; He interpreted the law; but His perception of the
claims of God went far beyond the constraints of the received
tradition. Jesus' complaint concerning the scribes and the
pharisees did not relate to their teaching of the law but to
their neglect of the weightier matters of the law – justice,
mercy and faith.[13] His concerns were the Father's name, the
Father's will, the Father's kingdom, the Father's glory. His
message was, therefore, concerned with the nature, the activity, the purposes of God. It required a radical transformation.
Its demands were absolute. 'No one who puts his hand to the
plough and looks back is fit for the kingdom of God'.[14] Jesus
took the notion of the kingship of God and gave it a new
meaning through the interpretation He placed upon it and
His identification of God's kingdom with His work. 'If it is
by the Spirit of God that I cast out demons, then the kingdom
of God is come upon you'.[15]

The preaching of the kingdom was accompanied by 'healing every disease and every infirmity among the people'.[16]
The question of His contemporaries remains pertinent: 'Are
you he who is to come, or shall we look for another?'[17] It
might be rendered: Are you the one who will bring in God's
kingdom? Jesus gave His disciples an interpretation that was
totally at variance with all popular messianic expectations.
He would merely point to the signs. He allowed others to
draw their own conclusions. 'Go and tell John what you see
and hear: the blind receive their sight and the lame walk,
lepers are cleansed and the deaf hear, and the dead are raised
up, and the poor have good news preached to them.'[18] These
are the mighty works in which Jesus displays the power of
God that is at work in Him. They are the signs of the glory
of the Lord, the majesty of God.[19] The prominence that is
given to stories of exorcism suggests that Jesus was perceived
to be in conflict with the powers of evil. Disease and infirmity
and demonic possession were the tell-tale signs of a world
estranged from God. Jesus' authority to speak and act for

God was confirmed by the sovereign power of God that was breaking into the human predicament through Him.

It is an extraordinary feature of the gospel tradition that the kingdom which figured so prominently in the public ministry of Jesus should have received so little explicit recognition in the teaching of the early church. Certain questions are, therefore, raised concerning Jesus and the kingdom and the early church. What was Jesus' conception of the kingdom? What was the relationship between His proclamation of the kingdom and the eschatological hopes of contemporary Judaism? What part did Jesus believe He was called to play in the inauguration of the kingdom? What was the connection in the mind of the early church between the kingdom and the death and resurrection of Jesus?

The kingdom of God is not a phrase that is frequently found in contemporary Jewish literature. Nor is it frequently found outside the gospels in other parts of the New Testament. The kingdom carries echoes of a nation's history and faith. It is a symbolic word of great power. It was for Jesus a concept which spoke supremely of the sovereignty of God. The kingdom meant for Him the reign of God, the active power of God, the sphere where God's sovereignty is acknowledged and exercised. Its Johannine counterpart is eternal life. It is doubtful if it is helpful to speak of the kingdom as an event which might be located either in the present or in the future. Jesus is not afraid to say that the kingdom has come among you;[20] and yet there is a sense in which the kingdom is yet to come in all its fullness.[21] The view has been challenged that the call to repentance was a vital ingredient in Jesus' proclamation of the kingdom,[22] but the way in which the kingdom was brought into the present by all that Jesus said and did required a response.[23]

Recent New Testament scholarship suggests that it is not possible to understand the early Christian movement without acknowledging the primary importance of eschatological beliefs.[24] These beliefs may provide the context in which phrases like the kingdom of God and the Son of Man must be interpreted. Jesus might be compared with charismatic leaders of popular religious movements that have an eschatological character.[25] His teaching can only be understood on the assumption that He comes as a prophetic figure, announcing the arrival of a decisive moment in history.[26] The messianic hope related to the fulfilment of God's promises for His people in history. There seems little doubt that Jesus anticipated God's imminent intervention. His saying concerning the destruction of the temple and His action in cleansing the temple need to be seen in the light of this conviction. Jesus' ministry cannot be understood without reference to the eschatological hope of Judaism, including the hope for restoration. One conclusion is that 'Jesus expected the kingdom in the near future, he awaited the rebuilding of the temple, he called the "twelve" to symbolise the restoration of Israel, and his disciples thought about the kingdom concretely enough to ask about their place in it'.[27]

The kingdom of God is inseparable from the person of Jesus. The ministry of John the Baptist had made a break with the past: 'the law and the prophets were until John; since then the good news of the kingdom is preached'.[28] But the reply that Jesus gave to John's disciples suggests that it is in His own ministry that the Messianic hopes are fulfilled.[29]. Jesus claimed an authority that is without parallel. He appears to see Himself having a unique role in relation to the kingdom. E. P. Sanders's conclusions are uncompromising: 'Jesus taught about the *kingdom*; He was executed as would-be *king*; and His disciples, after His death, expected Him to return to establish the *kingdom*. These points are indisputable. Almost equally indisputable is the fact that the disciples thought that they would have some role in the kingdom. We should, I think, accept the obvious: Jesus taught His disciples that He himself would play the principal role in the kingdom'.[30]

Jesus retained to the end the idea of the kingdom that had been so central in His Galilean teaching: 'I shall not drink again of this fruit of the vine until that day when I drink it new with you in my Father's kingdom'.[31] Sanders makes connections between Jesus' proclamation of the kingdom, His understanding of God's purposes for Himself and for His people, the reasons for His death, and the beginnings of the

Christian movement.[32] But to what extent did the apostles in their earliest teaching reflect the tradition of Jesus Himself? The proclamation of the early church took shape within the framework of Jewish eschatological hope, but there was one new and distinctive feature – God had acted in the death and resurrection of Jesus to initiate the new and final age. It was in the darkness of His passion that Jesus entered fully into His possession of the kingdom. 'In His dying on the cross the Christian imagination has seen the message and the man as a marvellously consistent whole'.[33] It was in the experience of death and resurrection, confirmed by the gift of the Spirit, that the early church discovered the sign and the guarantee of God's deliverance.

# Chapter 13

# Jesus and His Passion

Jesus' proclamation of the kingdom of God cannot be understood apart from the eschatological hopes of contemporary Judaism. The expectation that God would intervene decisively was not fulfilled in the way that had been anticipated by Jesus. The early church saw God's power at work in the death and resurrection of Jesus, but eschatology continued to provide the framework within which the good news of what God had done in Jesus could be proclaimed. The new age had been inaugurated but the time of fulfilment was still awaited.

There are questions, however, to be addressed concerning the meaning and the place that should be assigned both to the message of the kingdom and to the bearer of the message in atonement theology. If Jesus spoke about God and God's kingdom in a way that was not fulfilled, is it still possible to give Jesus the unique place that He occupies in the Christian understanding of salvation?

It is entirely legitimate to suggest that Jesus was correct in all that He had to say but that His message was fulfilled by God in a way that He could not have anticipated. The shape and form of His eschatology are subordinate to His proclamation of God's decisive intervention in righteousness and judgement to establish a new covenant with His people.

It is in the cross that Christian theology finds the completion of Jesus' work. The early church was only able to understand the cross in the light of the resurrection; but it was in the corporate experience of death and resurrection that the meaning of the cross and of all that had gone before was understood and related.

The death of Jesus was a judicial execution. The conflict appears to have been with His Jewish contemporaries, but the condemnation to death by crucifixion was a Roman decision. To the scribes and pharisees, the guardians of the Jewish law and tradition, Jesus was guilty of blasphemy. To the Roman authorities, informed and encouraged by the chief priests and the elders and the scribes, Jesus was guilty of kingly pretensions, of civil disorder. The penalty for blasphemy was stoning. It would seem that the priestly aristocracy of Jerusalem took the decisive initiative in securing His condemnation. The manner in which He had proclaimed the kingdom of God can only have strengthened the resolve of those who wished to destroy Him. It appears that the charges of blasphemy, kingly pretension and civil disorder were brought together to secure His death by crucifixion.

It is one of the ironies of the crucifixion that the actual form of death — seen from the standpoint of the Jewish tradition — should put Jesus totally outside the kingdom He proclaimed. He stands accursed by God.[1] But the judgement of Christian faith is that in His passion Jesus carries forward and brings to a dramatic conclusion His proclamation of the kingdom. It is here that He enters most fully into the human predicament, standing over and against all that makes for death and not for life. It is in His passion that God's dramatic and decisive intervention takes place in history as Jesus takes to Himself the messianic woes that herald the breaking-in of the kingdom.

It is not possible to enter the mind of Jesus and discover what the passion meant for Him; but there are several strands in the tradition that can be identified.

First, there is a conviction in the gospel narrative that the passion is within the purposes of God. This finds expression in the sense of inevitability that surrounds the action. Jesus rebukes those who would inhibit the woman from anointing Him: 'She has done what she could; she has anointed my body beforehand for burying'.[2] Jesus reminds His disciples at the Last Supper that 'the Son of Man goes as it is written of Him'.[3] Jesus challenges those who came to arrest Him: 'Day after day I sat in the temple teaching, and you did not seize me. All this has taken place, that the scriptures of the prophets might be fulfilled'.[4] Rejection and suffering appear to be recognised and accepted as part of the divine plan. They pick up the themes of apocalyptic or eschatological suffering that are to be found within the traditions of Judaism. They provide the necessary context for God's act of divine vindication.

Secondly, the proclamation of the kingdom appears to encompass the passion. Jesus had a unique role in relation to the kingdom. It was being proclaimed and inaugurated in His own person, in His teaching and in His mighty works. Jesus does not appear to have used the term *the Christ* in relation to Himself. He preferred to speak of Himself as *the Son of Man*. But Simon Peter's confession at Caesarea Philippi introduced a new dimension in His dealings with the twelve. 'From that time Jesus began to show His disciples that He must go to Jerusalem and suffer many things from the elders and chief priests and scribes and be killed, and on the third day be raised'.[5] These words are repeated in various forms in different situations – after the Mount of Transfiguration and on the journey to Jerusalem – but there is another word in which Jesus, drawing upon the ancient symbols of fire and water, speaks of the compulsion that is part of His preaching of the kingdom, a compulsion that appears to include the passion. 'I came to cast fire upon the earth; and would that it were already kindled! I have a baptism to be baptised with; and how I am constrained until it is accomplished!'.[6] It is the fourth gospel which makes the connection between the cross and all that Jesus had lived and worked for in His preaching of the kingdom – the Father's name, the Father's glory. 'Now is my soul troubled. And what shall I say? "Father, save me from this hour"? No, for this purpose I have come to this hour. Father, glorify thy name.' Then a voice came from heaven, 'I have glorified it, and I will glorify it again.'[7]

Thirdly, there is a notable emphasis upon the representative suffering of the Son of Man: 'For the Son of Man came also not to be served but to serve, and to give His life as a ransom for many'.[8] There is a general consensus that the use of the title *Son of Man* is derived primarily from the seventh

chapter of the Book of Daniel where it is used in an eschatological context.[9] But an examination of the language of this
particular verse in St Mark's gospel does not necessarily lead
to the conclusion that this word points clearly to Isaiah 53.[10]
It is a matter of conjecture whether Jesus interpreted His
ministry in terms of the Suffering Servant of Deutero-Isaiah.
It has been suggested that although there are echoes of the
Suffering Servant in the gospel narratives there is only one
explicit reference: 'this scripture must be fulfilled in me, "and
he was reckoned with transgressors"';[11] and that if the
identification of Jesus with the portrait of the Servant had
been the work of the early church, then the interpretation
would have been written far more strongly into the gospel
tradition.[12] It is acknowledged that there is no text from
pre-Christian Judaism which speaks clearly of the suffering
of the Messiah on the basis of the Servant passage of Isaiah
53, but that the possibility of such a tradition cannot be ruled
out.[13] Certainly it is clear that Isaiah 53 influenced the form
of the earliest teaching of the church;[14] and this view has
been endorsed by an analysis of the influence of the Servant
passages on the ideas of vicarious suffering in the gospels.[15]

Fourthly, there are hints in the gospel tradition that Jesus
saw His death – like His preaching of the kingdom – as a
time of judgement. The idea of judgement runs throughout
the scriptures of the Old and New Testament. It is a prominent feature of the ministry of John the Baptist. It gives to
Jesus' proclamation of the kingdom the note of urgency
which is present from the beginning as Jesus pointed men
beyond the present age to the judgement that belongs to God.
The relationship between the eschatology of the kingdom
message, the theme of judgement, and the crucifixion is established by Jesus Himself. It is present in the parable of the
vineyard.[16] It is to be heard in Jesus' words to the women of
Jerusalem.[17] It is to be found triumphantly in the fourth
gospel: 'Now is the judgement of this world, now shall the
rulers of this world be cast out; and I, when I am lifted up
from the earth, will draw all men to myself'.[18]

Fifthly, there are hints that Jesus attempted to draw others
with Him into some fuller understanding both of the kingdom

and of the meaning of the passion. The preaching of the kingdom invited a response. 'If any man would come after me, let him deny himself and take up his cross and follow me. For whoever would save his life will lose it; and whoever loses his life for my sake and the gospel's will save it.'[19] Jesus' reply to James and John when they had asked that they might be seated with Him in glory suggests that they too might ultimately share in His sacrifice. 'The cup that I drink you will drink; and with the baptism with which I am baptised you will be baptised'.[20] The words that are spoken by Jesus at the Last Supper lend themselves to more than one interpretation, but if it is St Paul who has provided us with the earliest and the most complete tradition then the invitation to 'Do this in remembrance of me'[21] must carry something more than the character of a cultic act. Whether or not the Last Supper was a Passover meal, paschal ideas and associations must have been present in the mind of Jesus. It is Jesus' words that connect the supper with His death and His death with the disciples. God's mighty act of deliverance, which lies at the heart of the kingdom message, and which the early church associated with the death and resurrection of Jesus, draws into itself all who will stand with Jesus and follow in His pattern of obedience.

Any understanding of Jesus and His passion comes out of that sensitive area where critical interpretation and prayerful reflection and theological exposition cannot be easily disentangled. It is one thing to suggest that the preaching of the kingdom had a primary eschatological thrust. It is permissible on the evidence of the New Testament to suggest that the cross was seen by Paul and, indeed, by others as 'the eschatological event of salvation'.[22] It is only with considerable difficulty that we can approach questions concerning the inevitability of Jesus' death, His expectations as He entered Jerusalem, the experience of Gethsemane, and the meaning of the cry of dereliction.

Jung's reflection on his life in *Memories, Dreams, Reflections* led him to conclude that 'Much might have been different if I myself had been different. But it was as it had to be; for all came about because I am as I am'.[23] This observation serves as a useful commentary upon all that is meant by the inevitability of Jesus' death. One scholar's analysis of the evidence, considered purely from a historical point of view, suggests that 'Jesus . . . did not seek death; he did not go up to Jerusalem *in order* to die; but he did pursue, with inflexible devotion, a way of truth that inevitably led to death, and He did not seek to escape'.[24] Was the final journey merely the pilgrimage of a faithful Jew determined to keep the Passover in Jerusalem? Did it represent a final attempt to confront the people with the challenge of the kingdom? Did Jesus look, in the light of Jewish eschatology, for some mighty act of messianic deliverance? The whole thrust of the gospel tradition is that Jesus' passion is no accident. There is a rigour about the statement that 'He set his face to go to Jerusalem'.[25] The words and the actions are those of 'One who knows what He must do and why He does it'.[26] It could be argued that the passion represents no more than the consequences that were bound to attend Jesus' uncompromising proclamation of the fundamental incompatibility between the truth of God and the truth of the world. But such an interpretation fails to do justice to the gospel tradition with its strong sense that the passion lies within the purposes of God. A critical assessment of the gospel narrative is bound to be open to the possibility that such a tradition has its origin in the perception of Jesus Himself.

There is one notable feature of the passion narrative which has a direct bearing upon our understanding of what was taking place. W. H. Vanstone in his book *The Stature of Waiting* has provided a scholarly meditation on the meaning of the passion. He takes the Marcan narrative as his starting-point and contrasts the activity of Jesus' public ministry with the passivity that characterised Jesus' behaviour after His arrest in the garden. Vanstone lays great emphasis upon the act of *handing over* in Gethsemane. He concludes that 'at a certain point in His life, Jesus passed from action to passion, from the role of subject to that of object, and from working in freedom to waiting upon what others decided and receiving what others did'.[27] The development of this argument takes a different form in relation to the fourth gospel, but Vanstone maintains that the transition from action to passion is of central importance in the presentation of the passion drama in at least two of the gospels.[28]

There is nothing here that necessarily conflicts with the conviction that Jesus' approach to His passion was conscious and attentive. The journey to Jerusalem, the entry into the city, the cursing of the fig tree, the cleansing of the temple, the parable of the vineyard, the saying concerning the destruction and the restoration of the temple, the discourses relating to the end-time, the words used by Jesus at the Last Supper all speak of purposeful activity. Jesus is portrayed as an active participant in a drama of apocalyptic dimensions.

These elements in the narrative merely serve to sharpen the contrast as Jesus moves from action to passion. The *handing over* that Vanstone has drawn out of the text – the passivity of Jesus as the drama of the passion unfolds – is brought into sharp focus in the silence that attends the prayer in the garden and the cry of dereliction from the cross. Three times Jesus prayed in Gethsemane, 'My Father, if it be possible, let this cup pass from me; nevertheless, not as I will, but as thou wilt'.[29] Moltmann attempts to capture the pathos of the garden. 'The appalling silence of the Father in response to the Son's prayer in Gethsemane is more than the silence of death. Martin Buber called it the eclipse of God. It is echoed in "the dark night of the soul" experienced by the mystics. The Father withdraws. God is silent'.[30] Could it be that the transition from action to passion is Jesus' response to the silence of the Father? Could it be that Jesus had been brought to the point where he knew that the truth of the kingdom for which He had lived and worked would only be made plain if He allowed others to take over and resolve the issue for Him?

It is, however, the cry of dereliction that brings us to the depths of Jesus' passion: 'My God, my God, why hast thou forsaken me?'.[31] Much has been said about Jesus' unique sense of being at one with the Father throughout His life and ministry. Attention has been drawn to His use of *abba* as the most familiar form of address that could have marked the relationship and to the one exception – this word from the cross – when He turned to the Father and failed to address Him in terms of such intimacy. Does this word provide a moment of insight into what appears to be the abandonment of Jesus by the Father? 'Man's last and highest parting occurs when, for God's sake, he takes leave of God'.[32] Meister Eckhart's word might well serve as a solemn commentary upon this word from the cross. The public ministry of Jesus had been marked by a triumphant affirmation of the kingdom of His God and Father. It is scarcely surprising that one interpretation of the cross should be not merely 'My God, why hast thou forsaken *me?*', but 'My God, why hast thou forsaken *thyself?*'[33]

The emphasis upon the abandonment of Jesus by God at Golgotha cannot be allowed to stand without qualification. The words of the cry of derelicion are a quotation from Psalm 22 and it can be argued that these words, which were recognised among the Jews as a prayer for help in time of trouble, can only be understood in the light of all that follows in a psalm which is essentially an act of affirmation in the power of God.[34]

But there is another way of approaching the question that lies at the heart of this word. It is suggested by a story that bears no relation to the events of the passion. Elie Wiesel describes how, as a young boy living in Sighet in Transylvania before the occupation by the Nazis in 1944 and the deportation of the Jews to the death camps, he turned to a man, Moche-the-Beadle, a man-of-all-work in the synagogue, to learn to pray, to be initiated into the mysticism of the Cabbala. Wiesel relates that, 'He explained to me with great insistence that every question possessed a power that did not lie in the answer'.[35]

The answer to Jesus' questioning word from the cross might appear to be abandonment. May it not be that we find instead a power that can only be discerned in the light of the experience of resurrection? Interpretation, reflection and exposition come together. Whatever purposes brought Jesus to Jerusalem, there is some reason to suggest that Jesus drew into Himself all the conflicts of our world, even to the point where it appears that He died not knowing how God would use His death. It remains for the fourth Evangelist to take us beyond the cry of dereliction to the cry of victory: 'It is accomplished'.[36] This final word from the cross might represent the judgement of faith. It remains to be asked if the one word provided by St Mark conveys the true meaning of crucifixion for Jesus.

The silence of God in response to the prayer in Gethsemane, the transition from action to passion on the part of Jesus from the time of His arrest, the abandonment at Golgotha as the cry of dereliction appears to remain unanswered might yet all serve one other purpose. There is reason to suggest that they assist an understanding not merely of the death of the Son but of the nature and purposes of the Father.

It is helpful to return again to Vanstone's exposition of all that is implied by the act of *handing over*. The words have consequences for the Son and for the Father. The immediate consequence is that Jesus 'creates a situation of which the outcome does not lie in His own hands and may be infinitely costly and painful and destructive to Himself'.[37] But if our Christology requires us to say that the incarnation was an activity within the life of God, that the Father was entirely and fully involved in the passion of the Son, that the power that is possessed by the question that went unanswered is the person of the Spirit, then there is a consequence in this act of *handing over* for all that we must say about God. 'If the truth of God is disclosed and the glory of God is manifest in Jesus, then the truth of God must be this and the glory of God must appear in this – that God so initiates and acts that He destines Himself to enter into passion, to wait and to receive.'[38]

The total exposure of which Vanstone writes so eloquently is the primary characteristic not merely of the passion of Jesus but of His incarnation and, indeed, of the whole work of creation and redemption. What Jesus does in the extremity of risk to which He hands Himself over is to display in the most dramatic form the character of God whose purposeful activity is marked by self-limitation and self-emptying. It would not be possible to dispute Vanstone's conclusion that 'of all that God has done in and for the world the most glorious thing is this – that He has handed Himself over to

the world'.[39] This is expressed in all that has been said about
God's relationship to man in his independence. It is implicit
in Farrer's portrayal of God making the world make
itself.[40] It is inseparable from the propositions that provide
the framework for a holistic theory of atonement. The truth
and the glory of God are to be seen in the patterns of interdependence and interaction, in the elements of necessity and
chance, in the competition and the conflict, in the appearance
of colossal waste. It is only in this complex of relationships,
which is God's way of working in His world, that the pattern
of life and death and life can be worked through, that the
promise of new life can be secured.

# PART V

# THEORIES OF ATONEMENT

## Chapter 14

# The Evidence of Scripture

One of the early fathers of the Eastern church described the death of Jesus as a mystery wrought in the silence of God.[1] All theories of atonement attempt to explore this mystery. They begin from the conviction that God's purposes of redemption and reconciliation are accomplished in the death and resurrection of Jesus. The fulfilment of these purposes will only be achieved when all things are brought into their unity in Christ.[2] But the cross is no mere display of God's loving purposes, a public declaration of the divine intent. It is the instrument of salvation. Christ crucified is the wisdom and the *power* of God.[3] It is through crucifixion and resurrection that God acts to heal, to make whole.

The New Testament does not provide a theory of atonement, but it gives a unique insight into the experience of redemption which was both the chief characteristic of the apostolic church and the starting-point for all subsequent reflections. The earliest confessions of faith stand within the tradition of biblical narrative. They provide an account and an interpretation. 'I delivered to you as of the first importance what I also received, that Christ died for our sins in accordance with the scriptures, that He was buried, that He was raised on the third day in accordance with the scriptures, and that He appeared to Cephas, then to the twelve'.[4] The repetition of the words 'in accordance with the scriptures' reminds us that Christianity has its roots in Judaism, but that the death and resurrection of Jesus had given a radically new meaning to God's covenant relationship with His people. Christian atonement theology takes account of the church's whole experience of Jesus. It does not merely supersede the requirements of the Jewish law and contain the promise of forgiveness. It speaks of the reconciliation of God and man. Its consequences are universal. It is a recovery of the wholeness, the oneness, of God's creation.

The apostles gave their testimony to the resurrection of Jesus with great power.[5] The completion of God's promises awaits its final revelation in the last time;[6] but the eschatological character of resurrection faith is vigorous and explicit. To affirm the resurrection of Jesus is to speak with confidence of God's purposes for His creation.[7] The experience of death and resurrection, confirmed by the gift of the Spirit, had inaugurated a new and final age. And there are wider connotations than the salvation of individuals or the abolition of ancient enmities between Jew and Gentile. The experience of alienation, of being in bondage, is shared by the created order. 'We know that the whole creation has been groaning in travail together until now'.[8] Here is the eschatological note of travail and deliverance. Death and resurrection come within the apocalyptic tradition in which the New Testament proclamation takes shape.[9] The lordship of Christ is to be acknowledged ultimately by the whole creation.[10]

The New Testament does not confine itself to factual statements. The interpretation of the cross and the meaning of redemption required the use of metaphors, analogies, images and symbols. These were drawn in large measure from the vocabulary of Judaism but they were able to speak to the whole Mediterranean world. Is it, therefore, possible to speak of primary characteristics within such a diverse body of literature, written to serve so many purposes over several decades? The canon of the New Testament is all the more compelling because it does not possess a uniformity of authorship, style and interpretation. It conveys an experience of redemption which is not merely rediscovered and renewed in every generation but against which the church is able to test its continuing life. It is the primary resource for teaching and exploration. And yet its creative potency is such that it permits new interpretations within the discipline of its own integrity, coherence and diversity. It is possible, therefore, to delineate various characteristics which must be incorporated within any exposition of the church's understanding of atonement if it is to be true to the evidence of scripture.

First, the work of atonement is the work of God. The divine activity is to be seen in the whole work of Christ. This was the burden of the apostolic preaching: 'how *God* anointed Jesus of Nazareth with the Holy Spirit and with power; how He went about doing good and healing all that were oppressed by the devil, for *God* was with Him . . . they put Him to death by hanging Him on a tree; but *God* raised Him on the third day and made Him manifest. . . . And He commanded us to preach to the people, and to testify that He is the one ordained by *God* to be judge of the living and the dead'.[11] The Christology and the soteriology of the New Testament belong together and they can only be interpreted within the framework of God's activity.

The *kenosis* of God is 'the revolutionary new element' in the Christian proclamation.[12] 'He who did not spare His own Son but gave Him up for us all, will not He also give us all things with Him?'[13] The cross is not merely a symbol of sacrifice or an appeal for obedient discipleship. One exposition of this verse from St Paul's letter to the Romans is that, 'What we have here is God's communication of Himself, the free action through which He establishes the effective basis of our salvation'.[14] The gospel is a message of grace and deliverance through Jesus Christ according to the will of God.[15] The pattern of the incarnate life is one of obedience; but the divine activity and purpose are to be found in the incarnation of Jesus, in His death and resurrection, in His exaltation, and in the judgement that has been entrusted to Him. Thus Paul is able to say of Jesus that 'all the promises of God find their Yes in Him. That is why we utter the Amen through Him, to the glory of God'.[16]

Secondly, Jesus represents all humanity in His act of redemption. Something has already been said concerning the role of Jesus as the representative man and the notion that in Him all things are united. Various words have been deployed to capture this aspect of the meaning of His death. His crucifixion has been called vicarious, representative and substitutionary. These words have all provided the subject-matter of extensive doctrinal debate. Their acceptability has been compromised for some by their close association with the legal metaphors and the sacrificial images that have been employed to expound the meaning of the cross. But none of these words can be lightly abandoned, and it may be that a holistic theory of atonement is better able to recover something of their meaning by its emphasis – derived from a general holistic approach to life – upon the extent to which the whole is contained in every part and every part in the whole.

The vicarious character of His death is related in part to the identification of Jesus with the Suffering Servant. The prophecy of Isaiah was, alongside the psalms, the most important text for Jesus and the early church.[17] The portrait of the Servant presented in Isaiah $52^{13} - 53^{12}$ has been identified as the source of no less than ten direct quotations and thirty-two allusions in the New Testament.[18] It was, moreover, one of the consequences of the persecution of the Jews during the time of the Maccabees that the notion of transferred merit – from the individual to the wider group – became an element in Jewish thought. There is good reason to suggest that the idea of people making atonement for others by means of their suffering and death was a familiar one at the time of Jesus.[19]

Any discussion of Jesus' death as being in some sense a representative act – 'He Himself bore our sins in His body on the tree'[20] – presupposes some appreciation of the biblical understanding of corporate personality which modern insights are able to endorse. This would have been understood by the writer of the Letter to the Hebrews who interpreted the death of Jesus against the background of Jewish sacrificial ritual. The high priest of Israel had a representative character. The people of Israel were present in his person. He entered the Holy of Holies and offered the sacrifice so that Israel might be accepted by God. This is the corporate personality that Jesus had assumed as the mediator of the new covenant. Thus, Jesus was called to taste death for all.[21] St Paul is also clear about the representative nature of Jesus' death. 'God shows His love for us in that while we were yet sinners Christ died for us'.[22]

It is St Paul again who explores the meaning of Christ's representative death in his exposition of the cross for the church at Corinth. 'For the love of Christ leaves us no choice, when once we have reached the conclusion that one man died for all and therefore all mankind has died. His purpose in dying for all was that men, while still in life, should cease to live for themselves, and should live for Him who for their sake died and was raised to life'.[23] The glory of this passage is that Christ's representative death cannot be interpreted as an event that is external to the life of man. It speaks not only of His representation of all humanity in His death and of His purpose in dying. It speaks also of the response that is required. The representative man demands the radical transformation that enables the disciple to say, 'I have been crucified with Christ; it is no longer I who live, but Christ who lives in me'.[24]

But is it appropriate to go beyond representation to substitution? There is a tradition in Christian theology which insists that Jesus is 'the entire guilt and the entire reconciliation'.[25] There was a large element of substitution in the sacrificial rites of Judaism, and the idea of substitution was increasingly dominant in Jewish thought at the end of the Old Testament period.[26] There is a substitutionary element in St Paul's assertion that, 'For our sake He made Him to be sin who knew no sin'.[27] It can be argued that substitution carries more deeply the notion of someone who enters fully into the death of sin. Dorner, the nineteenth century German Lutheran theologian, identified the substitutionary forces at work in the created order and in human relationships which enable us to identify Jesus as the Second Adam who becomes not merely the representative of humanity before God but the substitute for humanity.[28] There is no reason to withhold the use of the word provided it is acknowledged that all these words – vicarious, representative and substitutionary – are allegorical and metaphorical. The truth of an allegory is representative not literal. Jesus is both our representative and, if it is desired to retain the word, our substitute in the sense that He stands as the living symbol of the God who empties Himself in love even to the point of crucifixion, and who takes to Himself and embodies in the person of His Son the creation for which He is responsible and which He wills to restore to unity in His own image and likeness.

Thirdly, the death of Jesus is portrayed as a sacrifice for sin. The ransom saying attributed to Jesus,[29] the Pauline and Marcan accounts of the Last Supper, the preaching of the apostles, the attempts to provide coherent expositions of the meaning of the cross in the Letters to the Romans and to the Hebrews all suggest that for the early church a sacrifice of profound importance had been offered in the death of Jesus. Paschal imagery is present in the fourth gospel: John the Baptist greets Jesus as the Lamb of God who takes away the sin of the world;[30] and the Evangelist's timetable suggests that the death of Jesus took place as the paschal lambs were being killed in the temple. This is not the reflection of a later age but appears to have been part of the earliest teaching. St Paul rejoices in the sacrifice of Christ, our paschal lamb;[31] and the writer of the Letter to the Ephesians depicts the Christ who gave Himself up for us, a fragrant offering and sacrifice to God.[32] The First Letter of St Peter speaks of the precious blood of Christ like that of a lamb without mark or blemish;[33] and the language and imagery of sacrifice is, of course, present throughout the Letter to the Hebrews. 'For the bodies of those animals whose blood is brought into the sanctuary by the high priest as a sacrifice for sin are burnt outside the camp. So Jesus also suffered outside the gate in order to sanctify the people through His own blood.'[34]

Sacrificial language was used in order to interpret the death of Jesus. The early church drew upon its Jewish heritage and the wider cultural environment of the Gentile world. The concept and practice of sacrifice were the means immediately to hand whereby the incarnation, passion, death and resurrection of Jesus could be interpreted. Sacrifice was the most intelligible and pertinent image used to depict the meaning of the cross. The sacrifice of the cross was an act of perfect obedience,[35] and Jesus' death was a single sacrifice for sins.[36] Some attempt has already been made to explore the meaning of sacrifice and to acknowledge the importance of the blood sacrifice in ancient rites as the means whereby life is renewed and restored. A similar emphasis is found in the New Testament. 'Christ also died for sins once for all, the righteous for the unrighteous, that He might bring us to God, being put to death in the flesh but made alive in the Spirit'.[37]

The connection between sacrifice and sin has been challenged on the grounds that texts have been interpreted in the light of uncriticised assumptions about the function of sacrifice.[38] There is undoubtedly an earlier understanding of sacrifice as the communal act of celebration. There is also a sacrifice of praise and thanksgiving which is the offering of a consecrated life. Spiritual worship does require the presentation of ourselves as a living sacrifice which is holy and acceptable to God.[39] But the Babylonian exile had marked a turning point in the Jewish experience of sacrifice. Old practices had been given new meanings as worship became increasingly centralised at the temple in Jerusalem and the festivals were associated with the decisive events in the history of the nation. Rites that had belonged initially to earlier patterns of social life became associated with the saving events in the story of God's people. Sacrifice could no longer be dissociated from an exclusive and self-conscious understanding of the covenant relationship. The shedding of blood had become an act of expiation and atonement.

There are associations here which passed easily into the mind of the early church. The profound conviction that God had established a new covenant with His people through the incarnation, passion, death and resurrection of Jesus carried with it the inevitable association of His death as a sacrifice for sin. St Paul wrote of our being justified by God's grace as a gift 'through the redemption which is in Christ Jesus, whom God put forward as an expiation by His blood, to be received by faith'.[40] The initiative belongs to God; the response is one of faith; but the content of redemption is expiation by blood. And similarly in the First Letter of St John, Jesus is set forward as 'the expiation for our sins, and not for ours only but also for the sins of the whole world'.[41]

The language of sacrifice with all its associations is deeply embedded in the New Testament, but it does not follow that what is to be found here is merely one theory of atonement which might stand alongside other theories. The notion of the death of Jesus as a sacrifice is so significant within the New Testament that no theory of atonement can stand within the Christian tradition if it does not incorporate the element of sacrifice. Differences have arisen in our understanding of the word because there are elements in Jewish and in Gentile practice – reflected in these words of scripture – which later theories were able to draw upon which fail to do full justice to the earliest and most profound meanings of sacrificial rites. The rediscovery of these earlier associations and deeper meanings may yet provide a fuller understanding of atonement; and yet the New Testament interpretation of the death of Jesus as a sacrifice cannot be discarded. The power of blood is a symbol that has passed into the vocabulary, the literature and the piety of the Christian church. It continues to evoke an instinctive response.[42] It is easy to lay aside the primitive notion that the life is in the blood. It is less easy to escape the challenge of a life that is given in sacrifice. 'Greater love has no man than this, that a man lay down his life for his friends'.[43]

Fourthly, the death of Jesus is related directly to the righteousness of God and the justification of man. The words, the metaphors, that are employed – reconciliation, redemption, justification, sanctification – speak of the effects of the work of Christ. 'For freedom Christ has set us free'.[44] The new relationship that is opened up for man can only be understood against the background of Jewish law. It is impossible to speak of justification without taking account of the sin of Adam, the condemnation of the law, the penalty of sin, the wrath of God. 'Then as one man's trespass led to condemnation for all men, so one man's act of righteousness leads to acquittal and life for all men. For as by one man's disobedience many were made sinners, so by one man's obedience many will be made righteous'.[45]

Jewish and Roman law have both influenced the development of Christian doctrine with regard to the death of Jesus. There is no reason to suggest, however, that New Testament writers took over *Roman* legal concepts in attempting to draw out the meaning of Jesus' death and resurrection.[46] The important concepts – covenant, judgement, mercy, righteousness – stem from a Jewish prophetic tradition which had provided a theological interpretation of the nation's history. The righteousness of God is related to Jewish insights concerning the divine order, the structure of life, and the relationships of men and women as God would have them be. The paradox that appears to be present in St Paul's treatment of the law is determined by experience. 'The law is holy and the commandment is holy and just and good';[47] and yet, 'the very commandment which promised life proved to be death to me'.[48] The law is powerless to save. 'For the wrath of God is revealed from heaven against all ungodliness and wickedness of men who by their wickedness suppress the truth'.[49] But St Paul, writing out of his own experience of deliverance, could say that 'Christ redeemed us from the curse of the law'.[50] Sin, wrath and judgement are all related in St Paul's mind to his understanding of the cross.

Sin is a theological word. It speaks of man's experience of alienation. 'Sin means basically separatedness, brokenness – inside, a sort of schizophrenia, outside, fragmentation which we define when we see one another, not as parts, members, limbs of one body, but as individuals contrasted with us'.[51] It is the universal experience of sin that St Paul picks up and takes as his starting point: 'all men, both Jews and Greeks, are under the power of sin';[52] and again, 'all have sinned and fall short of the glory of God'.[53] Sin can never be exclusively personal. Such are the dynamics of all relationships. There is a solidarity in our experience of sin and of its consequences. The corporate sense of sin is dominant in the Old Testament. It is the whole life of the community which is impoverished and placed in jeopardy. Judgement is discerned not merely in the suffering of the individual, but in the rise and fall of nations.

The wrath of God has been interpreted – especially in traditional Protestant theology – as the judgement of God upon the sin of man. C. H. Dodd has attempted to introduce a new dimension in which, pointing back to the insights of the psalmist and of the prophets, he sees the judgement of God worked out in the events of the nation's life and argues that 'the "wrath of God" is not God's personal response to sin and evil but part of an inevitable "cause and effect" in a moral universe.'[54] Frances Young challenges both interpretations and argues that the phrase speaks of 'the eschatological woes, the great cataclysm of agony, destruction and disaster which has begun to afflict the creation . . . a cataclysm which would nevertheless be the "birth-pangs" of the new age'.[55] Dodd and Young bring in corporate and cosmic dimensions which serve to delineate the context within which the personal experience of fragmentation, sin, suffering and destruction must be set; and yet it is doubtful if these mechanical and eschatological interpretations of the wrath of God do justice to the evidence of scripture. It is necessary to retain the distinctive element within the traditions of Judaism and Christianity that personal responsibility and accountability are inseparable from the freedom of God's creation. The wrath of God carries with it in the New Testament a strong sense of the judgement of a righteous God upon the personal and corporate sin of mankind.

And yet it is all grace! It is faith that justifies,[56] but the promise of the fullness of redemption is the free gift of God. 'Therefore, since we are justified by faith, we have peace with God through our Lord Jesus Christ. Through Him we have obtained access to this grace in which we stand, and we rejoice in our hope of sharing the glory of God.'[57] It is impossible to escape the legal connotations that abound in the Pauline exposition, but they are set firmly within the experience of deliverance, freedom and redemption.

Fifthly, the death of Jesus invites our active participation. The cross requires a response. Jesus' preaching of the kingdom had included, for those who could hear, the call to enter into life. The earliest preaching of the apostolic church concluded with the challenge to repent and be baptised in the name of Jesus Christ for the forgiveness of sins.[58] It is part of the mystery of atonement that the Christian disciple is called to re-present the pattern of the Lord's obedience. It is not merely a participation in His death and resurrection. It is a participation in His life. 'For you have died and your life is hid with Christ in God.'[59] And the benefits of Christ's incarnate life, passion, death and resurrection are to be appropriated by grace though the response of faith. The divine purpose is mature manhood, measured by nothing less than the full stature of Christ Himself.[60] The evidence of scripture includes narrative and interpretation; it provides a theological exegesis which draws upon the insights of Judaism and the experience of the Mediterranean world; it has its own distinctive emphases. And yet its predominant characteristic is the experience of redemption. The meaning of the cross is to be found in Christian discipleship.

*Chapter 15*

# Theories of Atonement

All theories of atonement are required to take up and interpret in their own fashion these dominant New Testament themes. The word *theories* can be misleading. There are many traditions within atonement theology which have a distinctive character, a main thrust. These traditions draw upon the insights of the scriptures, the traditions of the church, and the contemporary milieu within which the gospel is being interpreted. They are attempts to expound the purposes of God, dramatically set forth in the death and resurrection of Jesus; but they do not always possess the rigorous uniformity of thought, the completeness, that the word *theories* suggests.

The Greek and Latin fathers of the early church were primarily concerned with Trinitarian faith and Christology. Redemption was not a matter of comparable doctrinal dispute. A variety of traditions existed alongside each other in which the conventional phrases concerning the death of Christ could be found. There was no coherent or developed theory of atonement, but it is possible in east and west to discern ideas and images that would come to count for much in the development of Christian thought. The main emphasis in the east in the writings of Irenaeus,[1] Clement of Alexandrea,[2] Origen,[3] Athanasius[4], Gregory of Nazianzus[5] and Gregory of Nyssa[6] is upon the incarnation. The work of Christ is God's act of revelation. Christ brings to men the full knowledge of God and of His law. His death was seen either as a sacrifice to God or as a ransom from the spiritual powers oppposed to God. By His death Christ has destroyed death and through His death and recurrection we have the promise of immortality. Salvation is seen, therefore, as a direct consequence of the incarnation.

The language of substitution, of sacrifice, of ransom, of recapitulation, is to be found in the writings of the fathers. Irenaeus and Clement of Alexandrea both speak of the blood of Christ as a ransom, although a ransom theory of atonement has been largely associated in the first instance with Origen. There can be little doubt that the early fathers are content in the main to reproduce the established words and images that are to be found in the Christian vocabulary, but the interpretation of the death of Christ either as a propitiatory sacrifice offered to God or as a ransom paid to the devil was undoubtedly influenced by the contemporary culture.

Frances Young draws upon the writings of Origen to show something of the influence of Greek thought as he wrestled with the meaning of the cross. Jesus is compared to those who died willingly for their country in order to check various disasters. 'For it is probable that in the nature of things there are certain mysteries . . . which are responsible for the fact that one man dying voluntarily for the community may avert the activities of the evil daemons by expiation, since it is they who bring about plagues or famines or stormy seas or anything similar.'[7] Origen directs attention, therefore, to the mystery of the power that can be released by one righteous man dying voluntarily for the community. Young summarises the theology of Origen: God is love; God acts decisively through the sacrifice of Christ to save mankind from sin; the blood of Christ is a ransom or aversion sacrifice which destroys the power of the devil and sets man free. It was in this way that Origen interpreted in a pagan culture the biblical idea that God removes sin through the blood that is given in sacrifice.[8] The ransom theory reflected the language of the New Testament; it resonated with the pagan culture of the Mediterranean world; and it retained for the death of Jesus a significance which is both cosmic and eschatological.

The ransom theory was generally taken up by the Latin fathers. The Greek fathers emphasised the power of the incarnate Christ to redeem and restore fallen humanity. There are affinities with Greek theology in the writings of Hilary of

Poitiers[9] on the sanctification of humanity by the incarnation and on the victory of Christ in His death and resurrection over death and the devil. The doctrine of redemption from the devil appears again in Ambrose[10], although the ransom paid to the devil takes on the character of a legal process.

It is possible from the time of Tertullian[11] to trace a distinctive Latin theology, deviating from the writings of the Greek fathers in ways that were subsequently pursued by the medieval schoolmen. There is greater emphasis upon the death of Christ. Words like *merit* and *satisfaction*, both of which were common in Roman jurisprudence, begin to appear in discussions of the relation of man to God. Augustine[12] sums up all that has gone before and introduces important new elements, especially in regard to baptismal regeneration. The idea of ransom is still present. Christ's blood is the price which was paid for our redemption. It is a ransom which both secured our release and ensnared the devil.[13] Redemption is release from the bondage of Satan but the idea of the death of Jesus as a ransom paid to the devil is not the main preoccupation of Augustine's atonement theology. Christ is the One who both offers and is offered in sacrifice. It is a sacrifice of expiation. It secures our pardon. Augustine's interpretation of the atonement does not possess the developed character of later theories but he makes the sacrifice of Christ the fundamental doctrine of the work of Christ; and in his doctrines of grace, justification, merit and satisfaction he prepared the way for a new understanding of the atonement.

It was Anselm[14] who took up after several centuries the notions of satisfaction and merit and developed through them a rational theory of atonement in his work *Cur Deus Homo?* The preaching of the apostolic church had focussed on the death, the resurrection and the exaltation of Jesus. Justification was the gift of grace received in faith. The teaching of the Greek and Latin fathers, mindful of the revelation of God in the incarnation of Jesus Christ and of the need to speak of His death in ways that would do justice to the sacrificial imagery of the Old Testament and to the experiences and expectations of the culture of the Mediterranean world, interpreted the death of Jesus as both a propitiation of God and a ransom paid to the devil. Anselm rejected any suggestions that the devil had rights over mankind. He set out to establish the necessity of incarnation. His treatise is an exposition of the incarnation. It becomes a theory of the cross. He attempted to show that the incarnation and the atoning death of Christ were necessary means of effecting salvation. R. W. Southern suggests that in this work Anselm and the young monk of Bec, Boso, who served as interlocutor in *Cur Deus Homo?* drew upon questions that were being asked in the schools on the continent, although the argument is developed along different lines.[15] The essence of Anselm's theory is that Christ made satisfaction for sin. The emphasis is shifted from ransom to satisfaction. It is the vindication of God's honour that is all-important. Christ alone is able to offer on behalf of all mankind the satisfaction for sin that God's honour demands and thus He secures pardon for all who will receive it.

This objective theory of atonement is monastic and feudal in inspiration. There are ambiguities within the thesis, but Anselm pleads the rationality of Christ's work of satisfaction with rigour, subtlety and force. The theory draws upon the use in the writings of the Latin fathers of terms and images taken from Roman law; but the idea of the satisfaction that was owed to God whose honour had been violated by the sin of man must be seen within the context of a feudal society in which lords had rights over their subjects and honour required satisfaction. The language and imagery of feudalism lay conveniently to hand. It spoke of sovereignty, of honour, of order, of a hierarchy of obligations and dependencies. Anselm brought to his work an utter abhorrence of sin. It cannot be freely forgiven. It requires satisfaction. Christ alone, perfect in His obedience, is able to represent mankind in offering the satisfaction that God requires.

It is suggested by some that this influential theory departs from the New Testament principle that the work of atonement is throughout the work of God. The role of the Son in offering satisfaction to the Father has the effect of separating the activity of the Son from the activity of the Father in the redemption of man. It is suggested also that whereas, in the writings of the early fathers, it was the death and resurrection of Jesus that had destroyed death and opened the way to immortality for mankind; in Anselm's theory of atonement, it is the death of Jesus that is fundamental. He fails to acknowledge fully the double process of death *and resurrection* in which the redemptive power of God is fully displayed. And this objection – if it can be sustained – leads to the further criticism that Anselm failed, therefore, to maintain the connection between eschatology and atonement that had been the dominant feature of apostolic preaching.[16] Southern suggests that Anselm's arguments did not find a ready acceptance within the schools;[17] but the practice of indulgences became popular from about this time and, although it cannot be argued that the practice was in any sense a direct consequence of *Cur Deus Homo?*, it was the objective or satisfaction theory of atonement that provided the doctrinal basis for the theology and popular piety of the medieval church and for all that it understood about the treasury of merit and the super-abundance of grace that Christ had established and can bestow. There were modifications and developments over the centuries but it is the objective theory that has informed the theology, the spirituality and the evangelistic thrust of the medieval church, of the protestant reformation and of post-Tridentine catholicism.

It is commonly argued that Abelard[18] proposed, by contrast with Anselm's objective or satisfaction theory of atonement, a subjective or exemplarist theory in which the emphasis is placed not upon the satisfaction that is offered by Christ in His death but on the change that occurs in man when he is confronted by the divine love displayed in the cross. It is doubtful if any such theory should be assigned to Abelard.[19] Indeed, Abelard's exposition of the cross is a very good instance of what has already been suggested: namely, that *theories* of atonement are often seen on closer inspection to be themes, ideas, degrees of emphasis. There are many traditional elements in Abelard's thinking: the idea of ransom; the notion that Christ bore the punishment of our sins; the message of liberation from the bondage of sin and the yoke of the devil. Abelard, alone among his contemporaries,

accepted Anselm's rejection of the tradition that the devil had
acquired certain rights over man.[20] It is true that for Abelard
the idea of satisfaction introduced an unnecessary element
into any consideration of man's redemption. God is not compelled to choose any particular means whereby He will
accomplish His work of atonement. The only necessity is
that which is inherent in the divine nature whose essential
character is love.[21]

The divine love, which is exercised in freedom and in
power, is the ground of the relationship between God and
man. It is the motivation both for the incarnation and the
atonement. For Abelard as for others salvation is from beginning to end an act of sacrificial divine love in which man is
set free from the predicament of sin and reconciled to God.
It is the action of God in Christ for man.[22] Abelard remains
within the Pauline and Augustinian tradition. Redemption is
the work of grace. The love we are called to have for God
and for one another will reflect something of the love God
has shown for us in Christ; but the love that is drawn out
from us will be a direct consequence of the transformation
that takes place in us through grace.

Anselm and the teaching of the schoolmen secured for the
cross a central place in the theology and piety of the medieval church. Abelard's exposition of the divine love failed
to secure general acceptance; but it has the great merit that
it goes beyond all interpretations of the death of Christ as a
legal transaction. It brings us back from law to love. It takes
up the Pauline emphasis that God's love commends itself to
us, in that while we were yet sinners, Christ died for us.[23] It
endorses the biblical insight that the saving benefits of the
work of Christ must be appropriated by each individual. The
sacrifice of love requires a response. Much has been made of
the inadequacies of the subjective or exemplarist theory of
the atonement, not least of all on the ground that it provides
an evaluation of the cross but fails to speak with sufficient
force of God's mighty act of deliverance and new creation in
the death and resurrection of Jesus.[24] The strength of the
objective theory is a clear recognition that something happened on the cross which was decisive for the redemption of

the world. It is doubtful, however, if the inadequacies of the subjective or exemplarist theory of the atonement should be applied uncritically to Abelard's exposition of our redemption.

The chief characteristic of protestant reformation theology is its firm insistence that man is justified by faith alone in the atoning sacrifice of Christ upon the cross. Notions of satisfaction and merit are taken up again, albeit in a modified form, but nothing must be allowed to diminish the work of Christ as the sole ground of salvation. 'All have sinned, and are justified freely without works or their own merits, by His grace, through the redemption which is in Christ Jesus, in His blood'.[25] The doctrine of substitution is carried to its full limit. Christ took to Himself the curse that falls on our sin. 'He has and bears all the sins of all men in His body . . . in the sense that he took these sins, committed by us, upon His own body, in order to make satisfaction for them with His own blood.'[26]

The influence of Augustinian theology continues to be found in the writings of the protestant reformers. Martin Luther[27] takes up and strengthens Augustine's teaching concerning original sin, election and predestination. He endorses all that Augustine has to say concerning the impossibility of faith or good works without grace. Luther's scheme of redemption finds its origin in the will of God and cannot be explained on the grounds of reason. His emphasis falls pre-eminently upon the death of Christ, but there is no new thought concerning its necessity or meaning.[28] It is in his insistence that salvation is by faith *alone* that Luther goes beyond Augustine's teaching; and, although faith is identified by Luther in certain places as confidence or trust, there is a doctrinal rigour and absolutism about his demand that faith is belief, it is 'a kind of knowledge which sees nothing'.[29]

John Calvin[30] picks up the main thrust of Luther's teaching that salvation by faith alone is the principal article of the Christian religion, and he stands firm in his insistence that, 'Our ground of pardon is the whole life of Christ, but especially His death.'[31] Calvin has provided in his *Institutes of the Christian Religion* an exposition of his fundamental beliefs.

The *Institutes,* which were revised and enlarged over a period of nearly twenty-five years, served as an index to his Commentaries; but it is the *Institutes* which have become the handbook of protestant reformed theology. Total depravity, penal substitution, justification by faith and predestination to salvation became the hallmarks of a rigorous protestantism which, while it draws upon much that has gone before, looks back beyond the schoolmen and the early fathers to the scriptures and, informed by Calvin's legal studies, provides a distinctive tradition of atonement theology. The human situation is utterly without hope: 'All that the heart of man can see is evil; he has lost, by the Fall, the power to will good. . . . All men are subject to damnation and from this Christ's death alone can save us'.[32]

Legal terminology takes its place again in the doctrine of the work of Christ, but whereas Anselm and his successors in the schools of the later middle ages had drawn upon Roman civil law and medieval feudal law, Calvin – with his repeated reference to the curse, wrath, punishment, death, substitution, surety, merit, imputation – turns instead to criminal law interpreted in the light of biblical teaching concerning the law, sin and death. And within this conceptual framework, Calvin – drawing upon the sacrificial principle that without the shedding of blood there can be no forgiveness[33] – identifies the death of Christ as an act of substitution and propitiation. 'Christ was put in place of evil doers as surety and pledge – submitting Himself even as the accused – to bear and suffer all the punishments that they ought to have sustained'.[34] It is this atoning death which enables God in His sovereign power to impute to us the righteousness that belongs to Christ alone. Calvin went beyond Luther in his emphasis upon the absolute sovereignty of God, but Calvin also insists that it is the love of God – the love of the Father and not only the love of the Son – that is the ground of our redemption.

Hastings Rashdall, writing from the standpoint of a liberal protestantism in the early years of the twentieth century, welcomed much that the reformers accomplished and bequeathed but examined critically its distinctive contribution to atonement theology – total depravity, the retributive theory of punishment, penal substitution, justification by faith alone and the imputation of righteousness. Its dogmatic theology, which attempted to remove the doctrinal corruptions of catholicism and return to the purity and discipline of scripture, was for Rashdall shaped in large measure by 'the traditions and ideas of medieval scholasticism in its last and most degenerate phase'.[35]

It is in the writings of liberal protestant theologians in the nineteenth and twentieth centuries that there can best be traced the outlines of a way of thinking about atonement theology which is subjective or exemplarist in its main thrust. The insights of biblical criticism, the awareness of man's biological evolution, the emergence of a new humanism, the understanding of human personality and of the dynamics of personal relationships, and a renewed awareness in theological writing of the love of God all contributed to a new emphasis in expositions of God's redeeming work in Christ. It is not possible to identify a distinctive theory of atonement, but the writings of successive theologians recapture some of the basic biblical and patristic principles and present them in new forms, reflecting something of what can be found in the writings of Abelard, and leading beyond the legal terminology and cultic forms of catholic and protestant orthodoxy.

Friedrich Schleiermacher[36] spoke of man's consciousness of God, of his dependence upon the Absolute, of his need to allow his awareness of God to penetrate every part of his being, and of the role of Jesus as the Redeemer who liberates that higher consciousness of God to which man is called. Schleiermacher provides, therefore, an analysis of the human predicament with its conflict between the higher and the lower consciousness. The initiative in the work of redemption belongs to God. Jesus is the archetypal man in whom alone perfect obedience is to be found from the first. Redemption or the liberation within man of his consciousness of God is still to be seen in some sense as an act of deliverance. This notion of human consciousness is taken up by Albrecht Ritschl[37] who interprets our redemption in Christ as being essentially a process of transition from the consciousness of sin to the consciousness of grace through God's self-revelation of His love in Jesus Christ.

The Scottish theologian John McLeod Campbell[38] might be judged in retrospect to have provided a link between German and English theologians. He rejected absolutely all penal theories of atonement. The incarnation, the atonement and our participation in the divine nature are all encompassed within the purposes of God's love. 'It is as having a place in the kingdom of God that we understand the atonement; for it is to our personal relation to God as the Father of our spirits that the atonement belongs; out of disorder in that relation has the need for it arisen; to bring that relation into harmony with its divine ideal is the end which it has contemplated'.[39]

R. C. Moberly[40] has provided in his work *Atonement and Personality* an innovative study of atonement theology. He recognises the need for atonement theology to be reinterpreted in the thought-forms of successive generations. His title betrays his conviction that neither atonement nor personality can be interpreted except by reference to each other. He makes explicit the role of the Spirit both in relation to the work of Christ and to human personality. He asks for an understanding of human personality and of inter-personal relationships as a means of illuminating atonement theology; and he seeks an explanation of personality which relates the self-identification of the Christian disciple with the Spirit of Christ without which atonement cannot be explained.[41]

Hastings Rashdall[42] and R. S. Franks[43] attempt to recover the primacy of love. Rashdall argues that it is only through human love that divine love can be understood, that love taken to the point of self-sacrifice is the greatest force in the world, that the regenerative effect of Christ's sacrificial love leads to a true love of God and man.[44] The centrality of Christ's sacrifice is not diminished but it is interpreted by Franks as 'the offering of Himself up to God on the cross to be a means of revealing the divine love'.[45] Atonement remains the work of God in Christ. The sacrifice of His death requires and enables the active response of men and women. And yet it has to be asked if these traditions of interpretation deal adequately with the questions that are raised concerning the reality of evil and the guilt of sin, the cosmic significance of the death and resurrection of Jesus, and the vital link that is present throughout the New Testament between God's mighty work of redemption and the beginning of the new and final age.

A notable development in atonement doctrine has taken place in the course of the twentieth century with the publication of Gustav Aulén's[46] book, *Christus Victor*. It attempts to distinguish within the great *corpus* of atonement writing a classic or dramatic idea which interprets the atonement as a divine conflict and a divine victory in which Christ fights against and triumphs over the evil powers of the world. The work of atonement is, therefore, a cosmic drama in which God is reconciled both to the world and to Himself. It is an objective idea of atonement in the sense that it portrays the drama of the world's salvation. The atonement is the work of God and it is a continuous activity.

Aulén argues that this is the predominant understanding of atonement in the New Testament, in the patristic period and in the writings of Martin Luther. The chief characteristics of his thesis are the primacy of God's initiative and activity; an understanding of the incarnation as the essential preliminary to the work of redemption; an exposition of the cross which places it firmly within the whole drama of Christ's life, death, resurrection and exaltation; a clear acknowledgement of the reality of evil; and a strong eschatological note. Aulén argues that this classic idea of atonement dominated Greek Patristic theology from the second to the eighth centuries, from Irenaeus to John of Damascus.[47] He insists that it was also the predominant view of the Latin fathers and, isolating the work of Anselm and of his successors as a doctrinal diversion from the mainstream of atonement theology, argues that the cross of Christ must not be designated as the saving event. 'Death is, indeed, the way by which the victory is won, but the emphasis lies on the victory'.[48]

Aulén rejects the word *theory* for this idea of atonement. Indeed, it is one of his objections to the classical statements of medieval catholicism and protestant orthodoxy that they attempt to provide rationally consistent theories. There is for Aulén a double-sidedness, an antinomy, which lies at the heart of the work of redemption. God in Christ engages in deadly combat with the forces of good and evil, and yet He is reconciled in His victory with the world. He is the reconciler and the reconciled. Aulén challenges the assumption that Luther stands in the tradition of Anselm. He argues that Luther recovered the patristic understanding of atonement: 'Christ delivers mankind . . . (from) . . . sin, death, the devil, law and the wrath . . . (but) . . . the nerve of the whole is the idea of the Divine Love breaking in pieces the order of merit and justice, and creating a new order to govern the relation of man with God, that of Grace'.[49] Aulén draws attention to what he judges to be the inconsistency within protestantism, attempting to reconcile the principle of justification by faith by grace alone with a juridical doctrine of the atonement. He rejects the humanistic perspectives which he finds in Schleiermacher, Ritschl and Rashdall.[50] Salvation remains for Aulén a comprehensive term which speaks of man's new relationship with God. The classic idea is expressed in many ways. It is essentially a cosmic drama in which God in Christ is victorious over the powers of evil. It is an eternal victory.

The idea of conflict has taken on a new significance in recent years with the emergence of liberation theology. This strand of contemporary Christian thought has not proposed a new theory of atonement but, emanating from churches which are attempting to work out the meaning of the gospel in countries that are often characterised by political oppression, economic injustice and gross social inequality, liberation theology has seized on the determining events of the Old and New Testaments in order to speak of deliverance and salvation. Marxist political theory and the analysis it proposes of the dynamics of human society have provided the language and the thought-forms of liberation theology. The key-words in its vocabulary are alienation, estrangement, praxis, liberation.

A seminal thinker in this new tradition of applied theology is Gustavo Gutierrez.[51] He writes against the background of the situation that he knows in Latin America. He sets the pattern of dependency – economic, social and political – that he finds in that subcontinent within the international framework of the class struggle. He argues the need for man to accept responsibility for his own destiny. He calls upon men and women not merely to reflect upon the world but to participate fully in the process of transformation. 'Sin demands a radical liberation, which in turn necessarily implies a political liberation. Only by participating in the historical process of liberation will it be possible to show the fundamental alienation present in every partial alienation.'[52] There are ingredients in Gutierrez's thought that are fundamentally biblical: the reality of corporate sin; the inevitability of suffering; the salvation that is mediated through the work of Christ; deliverance; the necessity of the prophetic word; and the call to costly discipleship.

It is against the background of his 'prophetic' interpretation of history that Gutierrez points to the liberating God who intervenes in history to break down injustice. The history of salvation lies at the heart of our history as a race. Creation and liberation and salvation belong together. In the events of the Exodus, Israel is liberated that she might become a holy people. This process is brought to its fulfilment in Christ who liberates from sin and creates a new people which potentially includes the whole of mankind. The Christian life can, therefore, be seen as a passover: it is 'a transition from sin to grace, from death to life, from injustice to justice, from the subhuman to the human'.[53] The work of Christ is central. He has set men free – potentially free – from sin and all its consequences; but the salvation that He offers is to be discovered and claimed in the contemporary scene. 'By working, transforming the world, breaking out of servitude, building a just society, and assuming his destiny in history, man forges himself. . . . To work, to transform this world, is to become a man and to build the human community; it is also to save'.[54] The eschatological promises of God are interpreted as the driving force of history. The action of God in history and the action of God at the end of history cannot be separated. 'Salvation – the communion of men with God and the communion of men among themselves – is something which embraces all human reality, transforms it, and leads to its fullness in Christ'.[55] The Christian is called to live out the prophetic concerns of the present and the unconditional openness towards the future.

## Chapter 16

# Faith and Culture

The evidence of scripture is the church's primary resource for an exploration of atonement theology; but throughout its history the church has adapted to society, influencing and being profoundly influenced by the world. There is a tension which runs throughout Christian history. The church has loved the world and hated the world. It has withdrawn from the world and attempted to take the world over. It is, nevertheless, through the life of society with its institutions and its traditions of law and order, its social relationships and social values, that the world impinges upon the church. It is through the thought-forms of a particular age that the church has struggled to express the truth of the gospel. The church's institutions, theology and ethics have all been shaped at different times by contemporary non-ecclesial influences.

This continuing process makes it possible to evaluate in their proper context the successive theories or ideas of atonement that have dominated Christian thought. The fact that particular words or images are used because of the contemporary setting in which the gospel is being preached does not invalidate them. It does demand, however, that there shall not be given to any one of them the absolute authority they have sometimes demanded. The church's history, tradition, temper and feeling will be important factors at any time; but the interaction between church and society, between faith and culture, remains vital. Whenever a major development takes place in atonement theology – often after a gap of several centuries – new thinking reflects the cultural climate in which it is set and from which it cannot be dissociated; but it also picks up many threads from earlier interpretations and thus provides the element of continuity within the Christian tradition.

The climate of opinion within which theological reflection and interpretation develop has been determined by various considerations. First, there has been the influence of secular thought, political theory and moral philosophy. It is possible, for example, in the early centuries to trace the influence of Platonism or neo-Platonism in the approach of some of the Greek fathers to theological questions. The political theory concerning the structure of early mediaeval society provided the vocabulary and the imagery that illuminated the theology of Anselm. Successive commentators have seen the influence of a new humanism in the writings of Abelard, of the protestant reformers, and of the nineteenth and early twentieth century theologians. The Marxist interpretation of history is a profoundly important influence in the writings of those who plead for a liberation theology.

Secondly, the church's understanding of the work of Christ has been greatly influenced by law. The church's heritage, rooted in the law of Judaism, required it to take very seriously the sovereignty and rationality and moral purposefulness of God's creation. Metaphors, analogies, images which derived from Jewish law and from the sacrificial rituals which had been codified in the books of Moses were taken by the apostolic church to interpret the meaning of the death and resurrection of Jesus. Biblical law, Roman law, feudal law, natural law, civil law, criminal law have all been drawn upon, and especially by the Latin fathers in the west in the early centuries, by Anselm, and by the protestant reformers in their exposition of atonement theology. It is not merely that the church has adopted legal terminology. It is far more that legal concepts have been employed to describe the nature of God's relationship with man.

Thirdly, the success or failure of the church in preaching the gospel has undoubtedly borne some relation to the psychology of individuals and of a culture. There are deep needs, hidden dependencies, within the human spirit which can be touched by the way in which the gospel is proclaimed. The meaning of sacrifice, the power of blood, the fact of dying,

the mystery of the divine love evoke the deepest responses.
The experience of sacrifice has never been lost. Blood continues to be a symbol of great power because it speaks of all
the absolutes in our experience, of the consecrated love which
is prepared to give itself entirely in death. There are so many
powerful symbols woven into the traditions of atonement
theology which speak not merely of different varieties of
Christian experience but of different psychological needs and
responses. The development of liturgy, Christian teaching,
patterns of personal piety, popular hymns have all been
shaped in part by needs that are very deep within the human
personality – individual and corporate.

Fourthly, it remains to be asked to what extent the intellec-
tual climate in which Christian theology is required to work
has been shaped at any time by the power structures, the
fabric of political life, the expectations and dependencies of
economic and social relationships. There is sufficient evidence
to suggest that time and again these things also fashion the
patterns of thought, the collective experience of an age, which
in their turn give a distinctive cast to the church's teaching.

The ransom theory that has been traced in the writings of
some of the early fathers owes much to the biblical insights
and to the contemporary culture of the Mediterranean world
in which the ransom or aversion sacrifice was believed to
liberate individuals and communities from the powers of evil.
It is right that this approach to atonement theology, which is
consistent with the teaching of the early church in giving to
the death and resurrection of Jesus a cosmic and eschatological significance, should be considered against the background of persecution in which the church, mindful of its
apostolic calling and of its gospel of new and abundant life,
was repeatedly reminded of its impotence and vulnerability.
It is doubtful, however, if the ransom theory could have been
expounded except in the context of a society in which slavery
was an established institution, in which masters had rights
over slaves, and in which it was possible to purchase freedom
by paying a ransom for a slave. The relationship between
the ransom theory and the institution of slavery was freely
acknowledged by Gregory of Nyssa, who applauded the jus-

tice of God's chosen method of securing our redemption not by divine *fiat* but by sacrifice.[1] It is difficult to imagine any network of relationships which could provide a more powerful image than slavery of the meaning of being ransomed, of being set free.

Proprietorial rights provided the background also to Anselm's objective or satisfaction theory of atonement. The notion of satisfaction had appeared long before the eleventh century, and especially in the writings of some of the Latin fathers who took their imagery not only from scripture but also from Roman law. Anselm's vocabulary and imagery were drawn from the relationships of medieval feudalism. Indeed, it is impossible to see how his notion of satisfaction could have been expounded except in the context of a feudal society in which crime was seen as an affront to the honour of the Lord in whose jurisdiction the offence had been committed. Within the theological context of sin and salvation, God is the supreme feudal overlord to whom satisfaction must be paid and in return for which certain rights and privileges would be guaranteed. It is a picture which was entirely appropriate – contemporary and intelligible – for the medieval mind. The notion of the death of Christ as a satisfaction for sin was demonstrated by reference to those acts of homage and fealty with which feudal society was so familiar. It was Anselm's great genius to bring such pictures into play to illuminate his teaching.

The appropriateness of assigning to Abelard the subjective or exemplarist theory of atonement associated with his name has been called in question. It remains true, however, that by contrast with Anselm he attempted to go beyond the constraints of law and the hierarchical relationships of a feudal society and place a greater emphasis upon the divine love as the ground of redemption. 'In dying for us He exhibited that love than which there can be none greater'.[2] The consequences of the divine love are such that man is set free by a deeper love at work within him to do all things in love and not in fear.[3] Could it be that Abelard's emphasis upon the divine love owed something to the tragic circumstances of his own personal story? Or was he drawing here upon a tradition of mystical prayer rather than biblical exegesis? Or could it be as several commentators have suggested that the inspiration was essentially secular and humanist?[4] It is possible to trace from the eleventh century a new humanism, a self-awareness and a creativity which were to find expression in architecture, in painting, in literature, in theology, in spiritual writings. Its full flowering was to come in the renaissance and in the scientific humanism of later centuries. It was to be taken up again in the writings of some nineteenth and twentieth century scholars concerning the work of Christ. It is possible that Abelard with his lively, independent and restless mind should be seen within the context of this new climate of thought of which he might be judged to be an early, harrassed and misrepresented prophet.

It was this new humanism which prepared the way for the protestant reformation. It demanded freedom of enquiry. It challenged established authorities and corrupt practices within the life of the later medieval church. It claimed the right to dissent. Its first significant ecclesiastical achievement was the translation of the scriptures. The great exponents of protestant orthodoxy in the sixteenth century carried forward earlier concepts of substitution, satisfaction and justification. The quiet scepticism of Erasmus[5] was abandoned but his desire to return to the writings of the New Testament as the basis of doctrinal exploration was never lost, and Luther and Calvin restored the fundamental Pauline concept of justification by faith.

It is impossible to know how much the thoroughgoing protestantism of the reformers owed to the spirit of the age. Erik Erikson's judgement is that Luther's emphatic assertion, 'Here I stand!', spoke for those who were determined to establish their autonomy, not only theologically, but also politically, economically and intellectually.[6] The independence that the reformers claimed on the basis of scriptural authority was set within the context of the sovereignty of God. The dissolution of feudal society; the long-standing disputes concerning spiritual and temporal power; the corruption of the medieval church; the emergence of questions concerning national sovereignty, independent jurisdiction and law pro-

vided something of the backcloth to the unequivocal emphasis of the continental reformers upon the absolute sovereignty
of God in whose will all law finds its origin. Luther acknowledged the authority of the state, permitted Christian people
to engage in its activities, but refused to countenance any
blurring of the distinction between church and state. Calvin
insisted, by contrast, that all true authority resides in God's
elect and that the church must seek, where it is able to do so,
power to manage and direct the affairs of the state. This may
not represent the formative influence of secular thought upon
Christian doctrine, but it is an extraordinary example of one
kind of authoritarianism – the medieval church or the uni-
tary nation state – being rejected only to be replaced by an
equally rigorous and absolutist concept of ecclesial sovereignty.

It was the work of some nineteenth and early twentieth
century liberal Protestant theologians which attempted to
break new ground. Their writing spoke of man's autonomy
in a climate of increasing secularism. The common thread is
a far greater emphasis upon man's self-consciousness, man's
dependency and the dynamics of personal relationships. This
new strand in the tradition required a new self-awareness
and self-confidence. The writings of Schleiermacher, Ritschl,
McLeod Campbell, Moberly and Rashdall should be considered against the background of a century which saw the
rejection of political absolutism, the establishment of new
nation states, the continuing demand for a liberalisation of
political and social relationships, the creation of *laisser-faire*
economies, the emergence of a new middle class with its
strong industrial and commercial base, and the influence of
secular thought. The initiative in the work of man's redemption remains with God; but the emphasis upon man's higher
consciousness, the attempt to demonstrate that reconciliation
is to be found in human relationships, the rediscovery of
God's love through an exploration of human personality all
bear the marks of a liberalism, of a new spirit of free enquiry,
that was to be tested in the upheavals of the twentieth
century.

It is the twentieth century that has seen the publication of

*Christus Victor* with its idea of atonement as a cosmic drama of divine conflict and divine victory. It is not self-evident that this understanding of atonement has been the predominant idea in Christian theology that Aulén suggests; but his work has enabled us to recover images that had been forgotten or abandoned as the earlier traditions gave way to the great theories of catholic and protestant orthodoxy. It may well be, however, that the popularity of what Aulén calls the classic or dramatic idea of atonement owes much to the fact of two world wars in the twentieth century, to the wholesale destruction of life that they witnessed, to the death blow that they dealt to the idea that man's capacity for progress is unlimited, to the recognition that the moral values of the most highly developed nations of the civilised world can be so easily abandoned, and to the failure of the churches to respond adequately to the theological and moral questions that were raised in their most acute form in people's minds. The twentieth century is able to understand the paradoxes, the contradictions, that Aulén embraces as a primary characteristic of his interpretation. It is able to understand the reality of evil and perhaps, therefore, the conviction that only the death and resurrection of Jesus provide the confidence that evil will not finally prevail.

The exponents of liberation theology make a direct connection between the work of Christ and the contemporary political scene with its experience of oppression and injustice. Gutierrez's interpretation proceeds from his analysis of the exploitation and alienation that prevail in Latin America. Iberian colonisation in earlier centuries and the development of a capitalist world market in which effective decisions are taken elsewhere have led in his analysis to relationships of domination and dependency which are manifested in unacceptable living conditions, unfair wages, starvation. Gutierrez is absolutely clear about the relationship between faith and culture. It is not only Christian theology but the conversion experience that is shaped by the human environment in which it occurs. He argues that there can be no authentic conversion which leaves untouched the political, socioeconomic and cultural structures, because it is they that inhibit our solidarity with those who suffer from injustice.[7] The doctrine of redemption that is to be found in liberation theology has the supreme merits that it starts with man's experience of alienation, it insists that sin is corporate and structural, it recognises that salvation is to be discovered in the contemporary scene, and it connects all these things with the eschatological promises of God which are the divine necessity worked out in history.

It is only in the obedience of Christian discipleship that the meaning of the cross can be discovered. The evidence of scripture, the theories of atonement, the interaction of faith and culture all bear witness to the Christian experience that salvation is deliverance, liberation, life. But no exposition of atonement theology can be judged to be adequate or credible unless it speaks about the life and death and resurrection of Jesus in such a way that these events are seen to reveal 'the ultimate significance and value of the temporal process as a whole' and to be 'the visible embodiment of the power by which that process is directed to its end'.[8]

# PART VI

# THE MYSTERY OF ATONEMENT

## Chapter 17

# The Mystery of Atonement

Atonement is a mystery to be received in faith; but the need to speak intelligibly of the Christian hope means that theories of atonement must be related to our experience of the world. God does not impose His pattern upon our understanding. It can only be discerned within the structures and relationships of life. Man struggles to speak of God's work, and the starting-point today must be a growing awareness of the unity of all things. It is in the exploration of the structure of matter, of the evolution of life, of man in relation to his environment, to his society and to himself that some insight is given into the patterns of interdependence and interaction, the elements of necessity and chance, the *motif* of life and death and life, and the promise of new life.

Truth is by its nature mysterious. It cannot be codified in a series of inflexible propositions which fail to acknowledge the insights and the contradictions of life. All theories of atonement draw freely upon contemporary experience in order to find the images, the metaphors, by which the mystery of redemption can be expounded. The four propositions which speak of the patterns of relationship that can be found in so many areas of knowledge and endeavour can properly provide the framework not merely for a holistic understanding of life but for a holistic theory of atonement, in so far as they are seen to reflect and to illuminate the substance of the Christian tradition – Trinitarian faith, incarnational Christology, the work of Christ.

A holistic theory of atonement proceeds from the raw material of life. Its claims are comprehensive. It makes connections with all areas of knowledge and experience. It is not possible to reflect upon the super-abundance of life without recognising the patterns of interdependence and interaction, the elements of necessity and chance. But the pattern includes a common experience of life *and death* and life. This is the process of transition without which the promise of new life cannot be achieved. Death can mean the physical process of dissolution. It can mean a fundamental reappraisal which is a form of dying. But *death* does not necessarily lead to life. Death can simply mean the conflict and the experience of fragmentation, estrangement, violence and self-destruction. But *death* can be a fighting-frontier which leads to life. This *motif* of life and death and life – seen from the standpoint of faith seeking understanding within the Christian tradition – is the fundamental principle, encapsulating the true meaning of sacrifice. This is T. S. Eliot's 'still point of the turning world . . . where past and future are gathered'.[1] This is the cross that is written with an iron pen and lead, graven in the rock for ever.[2]

A holistic theory of atonement is a *theory* in the true sense of the word: namely, it proceeds on the basis of principles which are independent of the phenomena which it attempts to explain. The principles or propositions which have been enunciated are borne in upon us by the world in which we live. They speak, therefore, from the standpoint of Christian faith of the rationality and coherence of a world within which God's purposes can be discerned. And the great affirmations of Christian theology are seen to correspond with them and to be illuminated by them. It is, therefore, entirely appropriate to take these four propositions as the key statements within which a holistic theory of atonement can be explored. And this theory can properly be called *holistic* because the Greek word *holos* speaks of that which is whole, entire, complete in all its parts. It is not possible to write atonement theology dogmatically without setting the redemptive and reconciling work of God in Christ within the whole context of Trinitarian faith, of God and His relation to man, of evil, of the work of Christ, of the purposes of God for His creation. It is not possible to write atonement theology apologetically without taking full account of man's search for wholeness which requires a new conceptual framework within which the holistic character of the universe is displayed. And it is difficult to imagine any word which can be applied more aptly to the Christian doctrine of *atonement*. A holistic theory of atonement is an entirely appropriate designation. Atonement is by definition a condition of being at one with others; it tells of a unity of mind and feeling; it speaks of the restoration of harmony and concord. To atone is to set at one, to bring into concord, to reconcile, to unite in harmony.

A holistic theory of atonement addresses the intuitive awareness that beyond the contradictions of the world there is some ultimate experience of unity – the *summum bonum* of all existence – to which we are drawn in the search for wholeness. A holistic theory is informed and shaped and disciplined by the insights of scripture and tradition. It stands unashamedly within the mainstream of Christian orthodoxy. Its *raison d'etre* is found in the conviction that our understanding of the contemporary world requires a new exposition of atonement theology and, moreover, that our understanding of atonement theology provides a pattern of interpretation for the contemporary world.

The first proposition speaks of patterns of interdependence and interaction. These patterns have been considered in relation to large areas of human knowledge and experience; but they have been used also to reflect upon the church's understanding of Trinitarian faith and incarnational Christology. This proposition has authority as a key statement concerning the dynamics of all relationships only in so far as it expresses the truth about the corporate life of the Divine Trinity. It can be judged to be a basic principle of life because it finds its perfect expression in the incarnate life of the Word who brings into a relationship of complete interdependence and interaction the divine and the human, and thus unites in His own person God's story and our story.

In all the areas of life that have been examined, this first proposition appears at first sight to do no more than describe in broad terms the *ideal* pattern of relationships that might subsist. But a mature and responsible interdependence can become an immature and oppressive dependence. A mutually enriching inter-relatedness can give way to a self-sufficiency which is determined by self-consciousness or self-seeking. An interaction, which must in the nature of things be taking place all around us all the time, can so easily cease to be the instructive, formative and integrating thing it is intended to be and can become instead the relationship of parties who identify themselves by their separation from each other. Political and economic relationships between the nations of the world, the ecological debate, the dynamics of family life, and the growing awareness of what constitutes a person's wellbeing all provide ample evidence of the universal experience that the ideal pattern of relationships set out in this first proposition is so often experienced as fragmentation and estrangement.

The second proposition speaks of the elements of necessity and chance. These elements are to be found throughout the living world, but Christian theology must locate them ultimately within the divine life. Necessity speaks of God's purposefulness. Chance speaks of the freedom that God gives to his creation. The interplay between necessity and chance is fundamental to all that must be said about God in His relation to man in his independence. There is a tension between what God wills and what man permits. The self-awareness, the freedom and the power of man are set within the pattern of God's self-emptying love in a relationship of joyful and creative tension. But the first two propositions tell not only of the ideal but also of the *actual* pattern of relationships that is encountered. The goodness of creation encompasses the fact of competition and conflict. The wonder of creation stands alongside the appearance of colossal waste.

This is the point where the disparity between the *ideal* and the *actual* patterns of relationship becomes so acute. If the propositions that provide the framework for a holistic theory of atonement describe accurately the pattern of all structures and of all relationships; if it can also be argued that this four-fold pattern is built so deeply into the fabric of life that it can only be judged from the standpoint of Christian faith to be the God-determined, God-provided pattern; how, then, does it come about that there has been *from the beginning* a disparity of such enormous proportions between the ideal and the actual? In speaking of conflict, it is not sufficient to speak of creative conflict. There is also destructive conflict. In speaking of waste, it is not enough to speak of the waste – the *embarras de richesse* – that is part of the glorious superabundance of life. There is also the waste that appears to be empty of all meaning.

There is a factor which defies all rational explanation. It has been identified as the alien factor, the stubborn element, the impossible possibility.[3] It is experienced as our tragic destiny and our moral freedom meet and match.[4] It is the inexplicable, life-destroying force that infects the creation and renders man impotent, vulnerable and culpable. It is the power that leads from life to death.

Christian theology identifies this power as evil. It is the inescapable fact that all theories of atonement must address. The starting-point for a holistic theory of atonement has been the search for wholeness. Evil is the power at work, deep within the fabric of life, which disconnects or disunites or destroys that which is whole or has within it the potential for wholeness and at-one-ment. It is entirely appropriate to suggest that the elements of necessity and chance have their origin in God. But the disparity between the ideal and the actual – the mis-match of our experience which is represented by destructive conflict, by the waste that is devoid of meaning – must be attributed to the power of evil.

The disparity between the ideal and the actual persists and can assume demonic proportions. Some organisms which have the capacity to adapt to their environment fail to do so. Some policies are pursued which, in spite of the knowledge and the power at our disposal, threaten the ecological balance which is essential to our survival. Some nations and individuals fail tragically to order their relationships with themselves and with others. Some actions – political and economic – conceived and implemented in the light of what is judged to be mutual self-interest can distort still further the gross anomalies of an international world order. Some people become, in spite of all appearances and expectations to the contrary, the hapless victims of tragedy through disease, violence, accident, circumstance. And those who stand in a long tradition of creative artistic work can deny the integrity of their vision and competence by providing the predictable, the pastiche.

This is the context in which a holistic theory of atonement must be thought through and worked out. There is nothing in this brief summary of the facts of our disordered state which diminishes the responsibility which each person is required to bear for what he is and what he does; but it is the redemption of *the world* by our Lord Jesus Christ which lies at the heart of the Christian gospel. Salvation is personal, but it is also social and cosmic. Such is the degree of interdependence that it has to be asked if God's work of reconciliation can be finally accomplished until all things in heaven and earth and under the earth confess that Jesus Christ is Lord to the glory of God the Father.[5] There are matters here that take us far beyond the complex of relationships in which life evolves and man pursues his search for meaning and belonging. There is a universal experience of estrangement. This is the tragic destiny, the alien factor, the stubborn element which requires acknowledgement and resolution. Evil defies and destroys the rationality and the coherence – the potential for wholeness – that are built into the structure of things. God cannot be the symbol of man's search for wholeness, He cannot be all in all,[6] unless evil is addressed by God and therefore taken up by Him – confronted and conquered – into His pattern of redemption.

Sin is participation in the power of evil. It is the consent – often given unwittingly – by which man takes to himself the evil that is endemic in the creation. Sin has its own common life. The relationships of interdependence and interaction that bind all things together mean that all share in the life of sin. It is an inescapable part of our inheritance. Evil and sin are destructive of the wholeness that we seek, of the atonement that God desires to give. Barth's analysis of the reality of evil led him to expound the meaning of *Nothingness*, the principle of total enmity to God. The character and consequences of evil and sin are identical. 'Sin is a monumental indifference to the totality of which one is a part and is otherwise without meaning'.[7] And all share in its deception of the truth, in its distortion of reality. 'The whole personality is involved. One cannot *do* wrong without *becoming* wrong'.[8] It is an attitude of mind, a corruption of the affections of the heart, a proud assertion of the will. It is a betrayal of the things that make for peace, and it finds its potency in the consistently repeated response to the temptation to be like God.[9]

Man retains his awareness of fundamental moral values, his innate sense of right and wrong, his consciousness of guilt; but there is an experience of alienation. The biblical metaphor which speaks most powerfully of this predicament is the wrath of God. It brings together all that the Old and New Testaments have to say about the holiness of God, His will for His people, the attitude of the divine love to sin, the consequences that must inevitably follow upon the evil in which all share, and the experience of alienation. H. R. Mackintosh speaks of the wrath of God as 'a huge, dark and commanding fact'.[10] One meditation on the cross conveys something of the meaning of this phrase. 'God's love is not unconditional. . . . (It) is like the wind of the spirit of life. It blows one way and one way only, towards fuller and deeper life for ourselves and the world. If we go in some other direction we find it in varying degrees against us. We experience the intransigence of things as though they meant to slow us down and defeat us . . . the Bible is so sure of this that it argues that we can only know (God) then as wrath.'[11] There is, of course, for Christian theology an eschatological dimension in all this. The wrath of God – like the kingdom of God – is breaking in upon us but it cannot yet be seen in all its fullness. The intransigence of things may be our immediate experience of the response of the divine love to sin, but Christian faith requires that evil shall be brought within the judgement and the victory of the divine love.

What has been called the intransigence of things can be experienced as suffering; but it is inappropriate to introduce penal categories and speak of punishment in relation to the divine love. There can be no accommodation between the holiness of God and the evil that is present in His creation, but the wrath that has been interpreted as punishment owes too much to a tradition of law which our experience as human beings invalidates as we cope with the deceptions of life and learn to accept and to suffer and to forgive and to build again and to know the joy of new life. Nor should it be assumed that all suffering is a consequence of evil. There is a suffering which, like conflict, is painful but creative. The power of sin, the experience of alienation, the wrath of God, the suffering which is a consequence of sin have often been drawn together in Christian thought with the fact of death. It is necessary to insist again, however, that death − like suffering − is not necessarily a consequence of evil. Death has become a symbol of evil and of God's judgement on sin; but death is also part of the pattern of life, an inescapable consequence of being born. It is part of the structure of our existence. 'We can blame man for his sin; and his sinful state calls for redemption. But we cannot blame him for those limitations that are his created condition and are therefore willed by God'.[12]

It is at this point that Christian theology is required to face the questions that have long since been posed. How does God reconcile Himself and His creation to the evil, the sin and the suffering that exist? What is God's guarantee that all things can work together for good in a world that He has made? Is it possible that evil and sin and suffering and death can be brought within the judgement and the victory of the divine love? What is the ground of our hope that God shall be all in all?

A holistic theory of atonement − like a holistic understanding of life − can only be explored within the framework of the four propositions that have been enunciated. The first speaks of patterns of interdependence and interaction. The second speaks of elements of necessity and chance. Both tell of the *ideal* − the God-given − pattern of relationships; but both expose the disparity between the ideal and the *actual* that confronts us in every area. The third proposition speaks of the *necessary* motif of life and death and life. Death takes a variety of forms as the pattern of life and death and life works itself out in the evolution of living organisms, in man's relation to the environment, in the lives of individuals and of societies, in the political and economic policies of nation states and regional groupings, in the negotiation of life's crises of transition by individuals, in the process of transcendence and transformation as new patterns of artistic expression break through.

The question that is asked in a variety of forms – Was it necessary for Jesus to die? – ought, therefore, to be considered within the context of this comprehensive pattern of life and death and life. There are many things that might be said about the inevitability of the death of Jesus. It should, however, be acknowledged in the first instance that there is a necessity about the cross if God is to be consistent with His own determined pattern of creation. But the cross is about creation and redemption. In giving Himself to His creation, God gives Himself – hands Himself over – to the pattern of life and death and life. And why? Because it is only in this process that the essential life-giving principle of sacrifice is to be found.

If sacrifice is the way that leads from life through death to life then it must have its origin and purpose in the life and will of God and it must be demonstrated to be so located. This is not to suggest that the cross is merely a demonstration or a revelation of sacrifice, of love, of judgement, of righteousness. It is *because it is a sacrifice* that it is the means whereby redemption is secured. This does not mean that the death of Jesus is an act of penal substitution, a satisfaction offered to the Father as a sacrifice for sin, in the sense in which these words have been used in earlier centuries. It does mean that in our state of universal estrangement nothing less than the sacrifice of the incarnate Son of God – offered in consecration and in love – can initiate the life of the new creation.

But what are the characteristics of this sacrifice that make it possible for us to speak so confidently of the cross as the instrument of redemption or atonement? Christian theology finds the fulfilment of Old Testament sacrifice in the cross of Christ. It is, therefore, still helpful to return to the composite, the idealised, picture of sacrifice that has been provided and to reflect in three successive phases upon the six stages that have been identified in the sacrificial rituals of ancient Israel.[13]

First, the worshipper draws near with his offering and lays his hands on the victim's head as an act of identification. The incarnation tells of God's activity in drawing near. Jesus represented in all its fullness the truth and the power of God. His public ministry spoke of God's desire to enter His world so that He might transform it. God became in this action a partner in our history which is also His history. This is the paradox of Christian faith – that the God who is high and lifted up draws near and becomes one with His people, participating in our story even to the point where He knows the corruption of our humanity. Jesus enters the ambiguities and contradictions of our experience and in His passion engages with evil. The cross is God's supreme and unconditional act of solidarity with the tragic suffering of His creation. It is in the cross that God comes to terms with the inexplicable fact of evil for the sake of His creation. It is only through this act of total identification – of becoming one with us and for us – that God can ensure that evil does not remain outside His judgement and His victory.

Secondly, the worshipper kills the victim and the priest presents the blood to God by pouring it upon or dashing it against the altar. There are important elements of continuity in salvation history, but it is inappropriate to bring to our understanding of the cross an attitude of mind which seeks to find exact parallels between the Jewish sacrificial system and the death of Jesus, to carry over from the old to the new covenant assumptions about the means whereby God accomplishes our atonement. It is sufficient to recognise the importance of blood as a symbol of tremendous power. Indeed, there are symbols on every side. Jesus is the pre-eminent symbol. The cross is a symbol. Blood is a symbol. Death is a symbol. The sacrifice that Jesus offered was a life of obedience but it found its completion in the cross. In His passion Jesus enters fully into our humanity and our mortality. If Jesus had not died in the brutality of crucifixion, He could not have represented man. The cross is the rejection by Jesus of the evil that torments the world. Nothing can diminish the centrality of His death. Death is for us a symbol of the power of sin. Death becomes through the cross the symbol of God's engagement which is the judgement, the forgiveness and the victory.

Thirdly, the flesh is burnt and is thus transformed so that it might ascend to God and a portion of the offering is eaten by priest and worshipper. The mystery of atonement is to be found not merely in the fact of death but in Jesus' transformation of death and of all that it represents by His death and resurrection. And this transformation is the work of sacrificial love. Sacrifice is about power. The power that is displayed *and released* in the sacrifice of the cross is the power of the divine love. This is the power in which the divine life has been lived from before the foundation of the world.[14] This is the power in which the divine life gives itself to the world.[15] This is the power which loves its own and loves to the end.[16] This is the power by which the Son lays down His life for us.[17] This is the power by which we pass from death to life.[18] This is the power from which nothing in all creation will be able to separate us.[19] But man is called to share in this sacrifice of the divine love. It is part of the challenge of the cross in Christian experience that it makes explicit the truth of our condition and invites a response. It is by entering ever more deeply into the pattern of life and death and life – the pattern of the incarnate and crucified and risen Lord – that men and women find their identity, meaning, wholeness, at-one-ment. This is the life of faith. It is the beginning of participation in God.

It is possible, therefore, to identify the distinguishing marks of the Christian sacrifice: God's activity in drawing near; God's participation in the human predicament to the point of total identification; God's engagement with evil, sin, suffering and death; God's crucifixion in the person of the Son; God's sacrificial love which absorbs and transforms and conquers and remains inviolable; God's invitation to participate in the divine life. And this leads, therefore, to the fourth and final proposition which belongs to a holistic theory of atonement. The Christian sacrifice brings us from life through death to life. To possess and to be possessed by God is to be born into a new relationship which has the promise of new life. This is the *intended*, the *desired*, the *God-given* relationship. Death and resurrection which form the distinguishing marks of Christian experience are used in a metaphorical sense but they point in the light of Christ's dying and rising again to the Christian hope which goes beyond all metaphor and simile to the new life which is God's free gift.

The recovery of the principle of sacrifice is fundamental to any understanding of atonement. It has been one of the concerns of theology in the twentieth century to reflect again upon the impassibility of God and the extent to which He shares in the sufferings of His creation and to what purpose. Abraham Heschel, the Jewish theologian, developed in the light of his studies of the Old Testament prophets a theology of the divine *pathos* which spoke of God's concern for and involvement in the world.[20] Nicholas Berdyaev, the Russian theologian, spoke of the tragic mystery of *suffering* which God Himself endures in the crucifixion of the Son.[21] Kazok Kitamori, the Japanese Lutheran theologian, argued for a mystical understanding of the *pain* of God in which we are called to share so that we might become one with Him in pain.[22] Miguel de Unamuno, the Spanish philosopher, developed a doctrine of the infinite *sorrow* of God as God suffers in all of us and we all suffer in Him.[23] Jürgen Moltmann took up again the theme of *suffering* in the divine life. He argued passionately that all human history is taken up by God into His history: 'There is no suffering which in this history of God is not God's suffering; no death which has not been God's death in the history on Golgotha'.[24]

These complementary approaches to the question of the passibility of God go far beyond the identification of God with His creation. They speak of the nature of the divine love. They tell of the cost of creation and redemption. They are expositions of the passion of God. The gospel of the crucified and risen Lord speaks of the divine victory. But is it possible for God to engage with evil to the point where He suffers and yet remains triumphant? Can God enter so fully into the torment of His people that words like pathos and suffering and pain and sorrow and death can be freely used without the destruction of His own eternal life? Is it possible for God's sacrificial love to absorb and to transform and to conquer and to remain *inviolable?*

Bernard Brasnett in his study of *The Suffering of the Impassible God* provides a way of looking at the problem which enables us to attempt an answer to these questions. God 'suffers because by that act of creation He so placed Himself that if man sinned it meant suffering for God . . . an impassible God may of His own free will lay aside His impassibility and allow suffering to come upon Him at the hands of His creation . . . yet there is an inner citadel where the destructive power of men can never enter, and where the Impassible remains impassible for ever. . . . As at the heart of a flame there is said to be a tiny space cool and untroubled by the outward flame, so here in God there is a divine calm . . . that no created thing can ever stir or shake'.[25] Brasnett's image attempts to portray something of the mysterious depths of the divine life. This is what Abelard called the love than which there can be none greater.[26] This is the centre of all being in which all things must ultimately come to rest and with which we are brought by death and resurrection to be at one.

Any understanding of atonement which is consistent with the New Testament must set the cross within an eschatological framework. This dimension is conveyed by three words in the Christian vocabulary that have been used from the beginning to explicate its meaning: judgement, forgiveness and victory. There is a necessity to bring evil within the divine judgement. 'Existent and persistent evil must somehow be finally excluded from the universe in which God's whole purpose is wholly fulfilled'.[27] Judgement is related to the holiness of God and the sinfulness of man. It is a significant theme. The cross is the hour of judgement.[28] The idea of judgement cannot be separated from Jesus' proclamation of the kingdom and from the conviction of the early church that God's promises are fulfilled in the death and resurrection of Jesus. But Barth reminds us that in biblical thought the judge is not primarily the one who rewards and punishes. He is the one who restores broken relationships and brings order into a situation of confusion and division.[29] The work of judgement seen from a human perspective is, therefore, concerned with reconciliation and at-one-ment. The eschatological note of judgement is related to what God is doing in His world and willing for His world. It is in this sense that the hour of judgement is the moment of truth; and the cross is the judgement of God on the evil, the sin, the suffering and the death that frustrate His purposes of love. There is a purgatory of judgement through which the creation must pass before the final destiny of participation in God's glory can be realised.[30]

It is the same idea of the restoration of broken relationships that is fundamental to the understanding of the cross as the means of *forgiveness*. There is the same relationship between the holiness of God and the sinfulness of man. And within the life of the Christian community, forgiveness cannot be separated from the work of Christ, from His death and resurrection. The sense of sin forgiven has been a continuing aspect of the Christian experience and this can only be understood in relation to the divine love. Forgiveness is given and received. The gift involves the passion of God's love and its reception requires the passion of man's penitence.[31] It is through grace that forgiveness is given and it is through the forgiveness that is given by grace and received in faith that man is restored, reconciled, made whole. To be brought under the judgement of the cross is to receive forgiveness. It is to anticipate in a life which is lived in God the final destiny of the creation.

Christian hope is confidence in the power of God; but Christian faith demands that this hope shall be related to God's activity in the world, to His purposes for the world, and to His power to achieve what He wills. The power to achieve what He wills is the *victory* of Christ's death and resurrection. Moltmann argues that this victory cannot be portrayed as 'the restoration of the original, good creation'.[32] He defines salvation at one point as 'the opening up of alienated man and this alienated world towards the fullness of the divine life'.[33] This is an inadequate definition of salvation, but it points towards the end and it is related to the conviction that God's creative work is to be found at the beginning, in

history, and at the end.[34] This definition corresponds, however, with Jarrett-Kerr's reminder of the teaching of Aquinas
that 'it is laid down in the natural law that the part "loves"
the whole more than it loves itself. Therefore man is made to
love God, who is his end, and only made to love himself as
pointing towards the end'.[35]

God's love for the whole – and for the wholeness – of
His creation requires the judgement, the forgiveness and the
victory of the cross. Man's search for wholeness leads to God.
It involves the process of life and death and life, the element
of sacrifice, the dying to patterns of independence and self-
sufficiency as the part discovers a new identity within the
purposes of the whole. The mystery of atonement gathers to
itself the whole drama of creation and redemption. And so it
is that MacKinnon can say that, 'What is realised in the
mission of Jesus and perfected in the Father's raising Him
from the dead is the very unity of God, the consistency of
God with Himself in relation to His creation'.[36] Man's search
for wholeness finds completion in the wholeness of God and
the wholeness that He accomplishes for His creation.

## Chapter 18

# The Sacrifice of God

The Christian understanding of atonement speaks of the continuous activity of the divine love, but it is focussed in the cross. It demands that the pattern of life and death and life shall be taken back into God. Christian theology identifies Jesus as the Lamb slain from the foundation of the world.[1] This poetic image derives from the conviction that the cross has its origin in the being of God, that the nature of His creation is such that the death of the Son is implicit in the act of creation. The mystery of atonement is hidden, therefore, in the depths of the divine life. 'It is as though there were a cross unseen, standing on its undiscovered hill, far back in the ages, out of which were sounding always just the same deep voice of suffering love and patience that was heard by mortal ears from the sacred hill of Calvary.'[2]

It is the divine necessity imposed by love which compels God to identify Himself with man to the point of incarnation and sinbearing crucifixion. It is necessary to speak in metaphors; but words have strengths and weaknesses. Substitution can so easily suggest that God acts on our behalf. Participation or identification convey more fully the notion of a God who, in uniting His story with our story, chooses to act with and through man.

It is the chief characteristic of love that it goes beyond itself, giving itself entirely, participating fully in the life of another or in all that is happening around it and yet retaining its own identity and integrity. It is in just such a way that Christian theology speaks of incarnation and crucifixion. The divine necessity imposed by love is God's passionate participation in His world. Christ enters the human predicament so that nothing might remain outside the mystery of salvation. The cross speaks of God's willingness to embrace mankind's capacity for self-destruction, the depths of violence and despair that we carry within us, the unresolved angers and torments of the human condition.

It is as though God requires us to meet Him where we least expect to find Him – in the darkness, the emptiness and the violence of our own destruction.

> 'He bears in His heart all wounds – those of the
> light that died,
> The last faint spark
> In the self-murdered heart, the wounds of the sad
> uncomprehending dark.'[3]

It is only in the light of such an understanding of the death of Jesus that the cross can be seen as 'a radical, a drastic, a passionate and absolutely final acceptance of the terrible situation, and an absorption by the very God Himself of the fatal disease so as to neutralise it effectively'.[4] Participation, identification, absorption: these are the words that mark the way that leads to atonement.

Elie Wiesel, a survivor of Auschwitz who shared as a young boy in the torments of his people in the death camps, describes the execution by hanging of two young men and a young boy in front of the whole camp. As he watched the pitiful spectacle, he heard a man behind him ask, 'Where is God? Where is He?' The two men died immediately but Wiesel relates how the boy remained there for more than half-an-hour, hanging between life and death, dying slowly before their eyes. As the spectators of the execution were compelled to walk in front of the boy, Wiesel tells how he heard the same man behind persist with his question, 'Where is He now?', and how a voice within him answered 'Where is He? Here He is – He is hanging here on this gallows'.[5] This is not the response of faith that some commentators have suggested.[6] It is the cry of death, the death of the faith and the hope of a Jewish boy, the death of his God.

But there is a silent voice that can reply to cynicism and

despair with an indestructible faith in the presence and the suffering and the power of God. One interpretation of the meaning of the story of Job is that 'the pious sufferer has no reason to envy the prosperous wicked. The wicked may have his prosperity, but the pious may have God; and in God have far more than the other'.[7] Those who have not experienced at first hand the brutality of this world can only begin to speak with very great reticence; but the silent voice of faith is heard in situations of great torment, and it speaks of the sacrifice of God in the God-forsakenness of man. It bears witness to the pattern of life and death and life.

Any discussion of the sacrifice of God is bound to take us back to the pathos, the pain, the suffering of the divine life. The love which gives itself entirely in death must be allowed to stand alongside the other symbols of God's activity. Indeed, it is the power of which the symbols stand possessed. The cross has been identified as a symbol and more than a symbol of all the pain that ever was – 'a kind of gathering of all pain, which becomes God's way of sharing the agony and ecstasy of His creation'.[8] God's mighty act of reconciliation reveals the ancient truth that only the wounded healer heals; and God heals only in so far as He takes to Himself our wounds.

Sacrifice recognises intuitively the necessity of the *death* – the giving up, the offering, the handing-over, the destruction – that leads to *life*. The Christian understanding of atonement encapsulates this universal principle of life that Jesus embodied in His death and resurrection. This principle was understood by the writers of the New Testament: the seed that is sown does not come to life unless it dies;[9] a grain of wheat can only bear fruit if it falls into the earth and dies.[10] The seasons of the year, the rhythms of the world of nature, provided the analogy that lay most immediately to hand to demonstrate the truth of death and resurrection.

This principle is to be found also in the experience of reproduction and in the care of the young. 'Throughout the entire range of organic nature one is impressed with . . . the transcendence of self in the reproductive process, which harnesses the individual to the purposes of the race, exhausts its reserves of strength, and often costs it its life.'[11] There is ample evidence from the world of nature of what can only be called callous behaviour, but there are also 'conspicuous acts of animal altruism',[12] especially on the part of mothers towards their young. The distraction display performed by ground-nesting birds when predators approach the nest provides a notable instance. 'The parent bird limps away from the nest, holding out one wing as though it were broken. The predator, sensing easy prey, is lured away from the nest containing the chicks. Finally, the parent bird gives up its pretence and leaps into the air just in time to escape the fox's jaws. It has probably saved the life of the nestlings but at some risk to itself'.[13] Is it too much to suggest that the pattern of life and death and life is lived out in these female birds? The instincts of self-preservation are abandoned. The claims of the new life to which they have given birth require, if necessary, their own self-sacrifice.

There is a third area where this principle of life can be discerned: namely, personal encounters with the traumas of life. These encounters can only be negotiated successfully if there is an honest acceptance of the truth of our condition. Conflict is an essential ingredient in the process. Suffering cannot be avoided. The rejected elements of our life – personal and corporate – have been called the shadow of our existence. Personal maturity requires a coming to terms with our shadow. This is the way that leads to healing and reconciliation, but this action contains its own death and resurrection. It will entail sacrifice. If crucifixion can be portrayed as God embracing the whole world, the response to the encounters that make up our individual lives must also embrace the whole of our existence with something of the integrity and steadfast courage of the Son of Man. It is only in this way that our personal and collective dying and rising can be lived out. The principle of death and resurrection is to be found not only in the world of nature, the processes of reproduction and the care of the young. It is to be found also in the confrontations and the victories that are part of the routine of human endurance.

The failure to participate in this personal and collective dying and rising has hidden consequences. Christopher

Bryant, interpreting Jung's thought from the standpoint of Christian faith, argued that individuals might exercise their freewill regardless of what God's will might be, but nothing could prevent the repercussions within each individual which are the direct consequence of disregarding God. 'I came to understand that to resist God was to run counter to the law of my own being'.[14] There is something here that comes very close to what Neville Ward called the intransigence of things. The judgement of sin is to be found in my free choice to run counter to the law of my own being. Sin is experienced as a deep sense of alienation from my true self and from the purposes of all around me and, therefore, from the life of God. The experience of sin is personal and corporate. The individual can know the alienation which he has inflicted on himself and which the world has inflicted on him. Sin permeates all structures and all relationships. The consequences of personal choices can never be entirely personal.

It is exactly at this point that Tillich is so helpful in drawing together the personal, the corporate and the cosmic dimensions in the judgement of sin. 'The most intimate motions within the depths of our souls are not completely our own. But they belong also to our friends, to mankind, to the universe, and to the Ground of all being. . . . Nothing can be hidden ultimately. It is always reflected in the mirror in which nothing can be concealed. Does anybody really believe that his most secret thoughts and desires are not manifest in the whole of being, or that the events within the darkness of his subconscious or in the isolation of his consciousness do not produce eternal repercussions? Does anybody really believe that he can escape from the responsibility for what he has thought and done in secret? . . . . The centre of our whole being is involved in the centre of all being; and the centre of all being rests in the centre of our being'.[15]

The argument comes full circle. It is for all these reasons that death is taken up by God into His eternal being. The cross is not external to God. It is within God. Death is taken up because in God nothing can be lost or wasted. The experience of alienation, the dimension of tragedy, the suffering that defies all reasonable explanation, the capacity for self-destruction, the rift that runs through man's nature – all these are taken up by God and are found to be in God. This is the meaning of the cross.

The activity of God in the passion of Jesus is consistently taken up by theologians. Moltmann helps us to set all that must be said about the death of Jesus within the framework of Trinitarian faith. 'God was not silent and uninvolved in the cross of Jesus. . . . In the passion of the Son . . . the Father Himself suffers the death of His Son in love for forsaken man. . . . God is acting in Himself. . . . God overcomes Himself. God passes judgement on Himself. God takes the judgement on the sin of man on Himself'.[16] In the cross God makes explicit the pattern of life and death and life. It is the pattern of creation, but it is not the invariable pattern. Death can mean extinction. Death will only lead to life when in the act of living and dying there is participation and identification of such intensity that the sacrifice of self-giving leads inevitably to the birth of new life.

In their accounts of the crucifixion of Jesus, the writers of the synoptic gospels speak of the darkness that covered the whole land from the sixth to the ninth hours.[17] *Death* will take many forms, but there is an inevitability about the darkness of death if the new life which is the victory of the new creation is to be secured. *Um Mitternacht* is one of the songs written by Mahler to the words of Freidrich Ruckert. No translation is adequate. It is impossible in any case to separate the words from the music and the voice of the soloist and yet they capture the darkness of the night in which God is discovered and embraced.

'At midnight I awoke and gazed up to heaven.
No star of all the starry host
Smiled down upon me at midnight.
At midnight my thoughts went out into the
bounds of darkness.
No light brought me thoughts of comfort
At midnight.
At midnight I noted the beating of my heart;
I felt a single pang of pain

At midnight.
At midnight I fought the battle of human woe;
But with all my power I could not decide it
At midnight.
At midnight I gave the power into thy hand.
Lord, Thou keepest watch over life and death,
At midnight.'[18]

These words might well have been addressed by the Son to the Father in the darkness that covered the land. But it is the darkness of death that leads to life. It takes the sacrifice of Calvary back into the life of God. The cross of Jesus is the sacrifice of God.

*Chapter 19*

# The Energy of the Cross

It is easy to affirm that the cross is a sacrifice in which from the beginning Christians believe God has acted decisively to accomplish the redemption of the world. It is less easy to speak of the energy that is focussed in the cross – released by the cross – leading from life through death to life.

The natural scientists and the mystics both tell of the energies that are basic to all life. A remarkable demonstration of the coming together of two independent and unrelated approaches to the meaning of life is provided by Fritjof Capra in his introduction to *The Tao of Physics*. He describes his experiences as he sat beside the ocean, watching the waves, feeling the rhythm of his breathing, and becoming aware of his whole environment as a cosmic dance. 'Being a physicist, I knew that the sand, rocks, water and air around me were made of vibrating molecules and atoms, and these consisted of particles which interacted with one another by creating and destroying other particles. I knew also that the earth's atmosphere was continually bombarded by showers of "cosmic rays", particles of high energy undergoing multiple collisions as they penetrated the air. All this is familiar to me from my research in high energy physics, but until that moment I had only experienced it through graphs, diagrams and mathematical theories. As I sat on that beach my former experiences came to life; I "saw" cascades of energy coming down from outer space, in which particles were created and destroyed in rhythmic pulses; I "saw" the atoms of the elements and those of my body participating in this cosmic dance of energy; I felt its rhythm and I "heard" its sound.'[1] This dramatic awareness of the energies that hold all life in being picks up in its own way something of what has been said about the nature of matter and the essential unity of life. It speaks also of man's capacity to understand and to interpret the process in which he is caught up.

The created world is a vast field of energies in which ordered interactions are taking place all the time. Man is part of this process. The natural and the human sciences both speak of the energies of life. Peter Berger gives us a picture in which the self is continuously created and recreated.[2] He is writing about man in relation to society, about the transactions between an individual and the wider community. His insistence that man can no longer be regarded as a solid, given entity[3] will be endorsed by those with a clinical knowledge of the interior life of man. Jung makes connections between physics and psychology, drawing a parallel between the various manifestations of energy – electricity, light, heat – in the world of the natural sciences and the psychic energy – hunger, aggression, sex – in the life of man.[4]

Jung has done much to inform us of the great reservoir of psychic energy that men and women contain within themselves. There is a notable story taken from Jung's clinical practice which gives a vivid illustration of the potentially demonic power of the psychic energy which transmits itself in secret to the world around us.[5] It concerns a woman who confessed to Jung that many years before she had killed a friend in order to marry the man she wanted. 'Consciously she had no moral compunction over what she had done. Such unease as there was appears to have been felt by nature and the atmosphere of the murder communicated itself to all around her through the damage it had done to her own inner personality and changed the climate of her spirit accordingly'.[6] But a succession of tragedies – the early death of her husband, the estrangement of her daughter, the abandoment of her friends, the loss of her horses and her dogs – brought her to a state of deep alienation which was tantamount to an exile from life and nature. It was in these circumstances that she came to Jung. Her confession made a profound impression upon him, and the woman's total alienation from life and from nature remained with him and was judged by him to be so important that he selected it for special mention in his autobiography where he observed 'that though one could keep such things secret in oneself, one could not prevent life from knowledge of it. The consequences of the murder one had done to oneself in the process found expression in the subsequent unease, estrangement and even disasters in the world without'.[7]

This encounter provides a brutal answer to Tillich's question, Does anybody really believe that he can escape from the responsibility for what he has done in secret?[8] Bryant wrote of the repercussions which must inevitably follow the free choice to run counter to the law of our own being.[9] Neville Ward spoke of the intransigence of things which is experienced as the wrath of God.[10] Many act wilfully or unwittingly in violence of life and of every principle that they or society hold sacred; and yet they appear to escape all the consequences of their actions. Few, indeed, would suffer such a total alienation from life as Jung has depicted in this instance. And yet it is fundamental to our appreciation of this reservoir of psychic energy which transmits itself to life that in the invisible world nothing is done in secret. Such is the degree of interdependence and interaction within that field of energies in which our lives are lived that nothing is lost. Every thought, every word, every act flows out into the mainstream of life. There is nothing in all the world that does not retard or assist the process of alienation or atonement.

The picture of the field or fields of energies in which all life evolves is one that is taken up in a partisan but imaginative way by Rupert Sheldrake.[11] He proceeds from the premise that our planet is a living organism; that the modern understanding of energy enables us to interpret and hold together our thinking about matter and motion and light and heat and electrical and magnetic forces; and that all organisms – regardless of their simplicity or their sophistication – are 'structures of activity, patterns of energetic activity within fields'.[12] His writing comes within the discipline of evolutionary biology. It postulates a new kind of field of energy – the morphic field – which is the self-organising principle of all systems at all levels of complexity.[13] It serves for our purposes as an illustration – no more and no less – of that picture of abundant life in which ordered and spontaneous interactions through interlocking fields of energies constitute the continuing process by which creation moves forward.

The all-important question can now be presented in this form: how are the great reservoirs of energy around and within us released for creative life, for wholeness? Jung spoke of the power of the living symbol to transform the inner conflict of our lives and to achieve order and reconciliation. He compared symbols to the great turbines which turn the weight of water that flows over the Niagara Falls into power and light and heat.[14] Symbols connect and bring together and make whole. Jung's analogy provides some insight into the power of symbols.

Jesus has been described as the pre-eminent Christian symbol. The gospels provide numerous instances in which He is the living symbol who releases the healing processes in those around Him in the course of His public ministry. But it is the fourth evangelist who assists our understanding of the energy of the cross in his account of the apparance of the risen Lord to His disciples on the evening of the first Easter Day, bringing together in a remarkable way the crucifixion and the gift of the Spirit. 'Jesus came and stood among them and said to them, "Peace be with you". When he had said this, He showed them His hands and His side. Then the disciples were glad when they saw the Lord. Jesus said to them again, "Peace be with you. As the Father has sent me, even so I send you". And when He had said this He breathed on them, and said to them, "Receive the Holy Spirit"'.[15] First, He showed the disciples His hands and His side. Secondly, He breathed on them and said, 'Receive the Holy Spirit'. What explanation can be offered for this sequence? What is the connection between the cross and the Spirit? The experience of life suggests that it is only when we make a decision with the whole of our being that we release the power which enables us to accomplish our purpose.

Laurens van der Post gives us a helpful illustration. It is prompted by an incident in the course of his expedition to find the primitive bushmen of Africa; but he reflects not merely upon that incident but upon his wider experiences of life. 'Often in my life I have found that the one thing that can save is the thing which appears most to threaten. In peace and war I have found that frequently, naked and unashamed, one has to go down into what one most fears and in that process, from somewhere beyond all conscious expectation, comes a fading flicker of light and energy that even if it does not produce the courage of a hero at any rate enables a trembling mortal to take one step further'.[16] The validity of this insight has been found repeatedly as men and women have learned to cope with all that threatens to destroy. Christian piety might well find in this picture a parallel with the Christ who, in His death, goes down naked and unashamed into what He most fears, and who in the process – beyond all conscious expectation – releases that saving flicker of light and energy which is resurrection life. It is as though in His death upon on the cross, Jesus released the energy of the new creation.

But is it permissible to make connections simply on the basis of one word between the energies of the natural and the human sciences, the power of the living symbol, the work of Christ, the sacrifice of suffering love, the gift of the Spirit, and the life of the new creation? It is a little over a century since B. F. Westcott gave a series of Holy Week addresses on *The Victory of the Cross*.[17] He recognised that we are all fragments in an organic, growing whole;[18] and he went on to speak of the subtle forces that come to us and go from us, witnessing to the vital unity of mankind.[19] It is necessary to turn to the insights of the mystics, who acknowledge the subtle forces, the energies of life, within a world in which 'every event in time and history affects in some measure the whole creation, since all the elements of the world are interdependent'.[20]

But what is the energy that flows from the cross? The Mahatma Ghandi, standing in a non-Christian tradition, spoke of the power of truth and love. His judgement was clear that love is the force that holds all things in being. 'Scientists tell us that without the presence of the cohesive force amongst the atoms that compose this globe of ours it would crumble to pieces and we would cease to exist, and even as there is a cohesive force in blind nature so much must there be in all things animate and the name for that cohesive force among animate beings is Love'.[21] The argument returns to the power of the divine love that is displayed and released in the sacrifice of the cross. Westcott spoke of forgiveness as 'the energy of love answered by love'.[22] It is fundamental to a holistic theory of atonement that the suffering love which gives itself in sacrifice is the principle of life, the power by which God acts to transform and make whole.

It is the living symbol which releases the energies that heal, that make whole, that enable us to become holy, to be at one. 'In a mysterious way the Man upon the cross retains His place in the human imagination as the timeless symbol of reconciliation through sacrifice'.[23] But it is not sufficient merely to retain the language and imagery of sacrifice in order to speak about the meaning of the cross. The cross is the supreme Christian symbol of the triumph of love in a world that is all too often experienced as grief and despair. It speaks of the promise of forgiveness, of reconciliation, of wholeness. But the pattern of death and resurrection must be discovered and reproduced. The promise of new life requires the obedience of lives that embrace the cross at the centre of their being. The principle of sacrifice remains. It is life and death and life.

There is nothing here to suggest that God's work of atonement is of personal consequence alone. Indeed, it is the energy of the cross – the life that is released by the suffering love which gives itself in sacrifice – which makes it possible to hold together the personal, the social, the corporate and the cosmic dimensions of redemption. Man's special responsibility remains because he is able by virtue of his self-awareness to bring into the continuing drama of creation all that he sees around him. But the distinguishing characteristics of man in his relation to God are self-awareness, freedom and power. If it is true that God's relationship with His creation is one of continuous participation and interaction, then there is a pattern into which man also enters – for good or for ill – by virtue of his freedom and his power.

The nature of man's relation to the created order is such that theological questions must inevitably be raised concerning man's capacity to retard the processes of redemption. 'If man, as the creature who is also co-creator, is in constant interaction with his environment as a whole, if he is part of the intricately inter-connected workings of the universe, then a disorder in man must produce some disorder in his environment. The theological theories of a cosmic fall hint at a kind of moral pollution. They suggest that man's sinful acts extend in their consequences far beyond what he normally supposes, and that they tend to frustrate and deflect the cosmos from whatever purposes of good God may have for it'.[24]

No one can begin to describe the way in which these intricately inter-connected workings of the universe operate, but sufficient is known about the interdependence of all things for us to understand that in the silent mysteries of life, the hidden depths of being, man's actions must have consequences which extend far beyond all that is seen or known. It is a corollary of this truth that man can also work with and not merely against the purposes of God, and can therefore assist the reconciliation of all things in the person of the crucified and risen Lord. Atonement remains the work of God. The energy of the cross is the life of the new creation. It is the power that will ultimately unite all things in Christ.

The idea of being redeemed, fulfilled, accomplished, brought to completion that is to be found throughout the New Testament encompasses the whole created order. The mystery of atonement incorporates the vision of a new heaven and a new earth. All things have their beginning and their end in God; but nothing can be understood without reference to the cross. *Crux omnia probat.* The sacrifice of suffering love continues its silent work of redemption. Atonement is the travail of the ages. It is made explicit in Gethsemane and Calvary; but the sacrifice of God is continually offered in the passion of the Holy Spirit, transforming the world into the image of the Son of God.[25]

# PART VII

## LIFE IN GOD

## Chapter 20

# Life in God

In the tradition of the Orthodox Church, the theologian is one who follows the path of union with God.[1] The knowledge of God which comes through mystical experience can be obscure and deeply mysterious.[2] There is, however, an awareness of grace to which the Christian tradition can appeal. It is exactly here in these moments of truth that Christian theology must show how man's most authentic experiences – the things that speak most powerfully of his humanity – are hidden in the mystery of grace and are the work of grace.[3]

The letter that was written as a post-script to *The Diary of a Country Priest* describes how the priest, who died before he could receive the last rites, the consolations of his religion, was still able to say to the friend with whom he spent his final evening, 'Does it matter? Grace is ... everywhere'.[4] This deceptively simple acknowledgement of the mystery of grace is in reality the confession of a mature faith. The conviction that 'grace is the Holy Spirit received'[5] opens up a world in which the Holy Spirit is preveniently and pre-eminently at work. And to share – consciously or unconsciously – in the life of the Spirit is to be caught up in God's work of atonement in Jesus Christ. But for those who stand in the Christian tradition, to live the life of the Spirit is to be set with Christ in His transition from death to life.[6] It is to participate in God's work of transforming the world into the image of His Son.

It is for this reason that theology will make connections with all that is happening in the world. If it fails to do so, it will diminish the God of whom it speaks. It is the conviction of Christian faith that the power of life in the world of nature, in the cell and in the organism, in plant life and in the animal creation is a reflection of the life that is in God.[7] The knowledge of the mystics that all life is one is finding confirmation in the work of modern physics which shows the world to be 'a system of inseparable, interacting and ever-moving components'.[8]

Bede Griffiths, drawing his inspiration from the religious traditions of east and west, finds in Plotinus his own belief that, 'Light runs through light and each of them contains all within itself, and at the same time sees all in every other, so that everywhere there is all, and all is all and each all, and infinite the glory'.[9] Griffiths traces this vision of life in the philosophy of ancient Greece, India, China and Arabia. He finds it supremely in the Christian doctrine of the mystical body of Christ where, rejoicing in the freedom of the Spirit and beholding the glory of the Lord, we are changed into His likeness as we advance from glory to glory.[10]

This is St Paul's way of speaking of our personal transformation by the Holy Spirit into the image of the Son of God. But what part is man called to play in the Spirit's work of transforming the world? Creation, incarnation and crucifixion speak of the extent to which God gives Himself to the world. Man has the ability to understand, to articulate, and to participate consciously in the process of transformation. The participation that is desired will have something of the character of God's wholehearted participation. It will be the response of the human spirit to the Holy Spirit. And in this endeavour we are united with each other and with God because the mystical body of Christ embraces – or, to be more correct, is potentially capable of embracing – the whole of humanity in the person of Christ until we are finally brought to the state in which, as St Augustine expresses it, there is only 'one Christ loving Himself'.[11]

The experience of the indwelling and transforming power of the Holy Spirit finds its most familiar expression in the New Testament concept of being in Christ. 'We, though many, are one body in Christ, and individually members one of another'.[12] The initiative remains with God, the invitation is to abide in Christ, the transformation can be likened to a new creation.

The experience of being in Christ reflects something of the Trinitarian understanding of God. The three Persons of the Trinity are not parts of the divine life which might be considered in isolation from each other. 'As in God each one of the three Persons . . . is not a part of the Trinity but is fully God . . . so the church is not a federation of parts . . . each part of her is identified with the whole, expresses the whole, has the value which the whole has, does not exist outside the whole'.[13] The Trinitarian model assists the understanding of atonement – of being at one – and speaks in a thoroughly contemporary way of our interdependence and essential unity.

The experience of being in Christ brings with it some understanding of the meaning of an incarnational Christology because it enlarges the awareness of what it means to be a person. It challenges the autonomy and the possessiveness that are the characteristics of individualisation. It is only when a person desires nothing for himself that he finds the depths of a shared humanity and becomes truly alive. The process leads back to the divine pattern of self-emptying love. The God who loved to the point of incarnation and crucifixion is the God of whom it might be said that He seeks to possess nothing for Himself; and yet the passion of His love calls forth the response of love.

The experience of being in Christ provides an understanding of sacrifice. The words *in Christ* are to be found in one hundred and sixty-four places in the writings of St Paul[14] and the passages which speak of Christ as the head of the body invariably associate this role with His death and resurrection[15]. The pattern of Jesus is to be the pattern of Christian discipleship. But it is only within the community of faith and worship and service that the meaning of sacrifice can be understood. The cross which is at the heart of God requires His participation in His world and our participation in Him. It is a relationship in which the power which is the life of the new creation can be given and received.

Mystical knowledge and practical experience complement

each other. The consequences of being in Christ involve the call to holiness of living, the rediscovery of our humanity and of our solidarity with each other, and the exploration of the mystery of atonement.

The call to holiness of living is the call to mature manhood, measured by nothing less than the full stature of Christ Himself.[16] This mature manhood will bear the marks of the cross – the crucifixion of the flesh with its passions and desires,[17] and it will yield the fruits of the Spirit – love, joy, peace, patience, kindness, goodness, faithfulness, gentleness, self-control.[18] The pattern of life and death and life repeats itself. Atonement requires that all shall come within the constraints of the life and love of God revealed in the death and resurrection of Jesus Christ. To abide in Christ is to keep His commandments;[19] but to live in Christ is to move beyond participation in the life of God, it is to become a revelation of His life. The victory of the cross is the cry of St Paul, 'It is no longer I who live, but Christ who lives in me'.[20]

The rediscovery of our humanity leads inevitably to a new sense of our solidarity with each other and with the created order. The experience of estrangement means that our lives are lived as individuals by distancing ourselves from each other. 'Each man affirms himself by contrasting himself with others. . . . But in the measure in which he is a person in the true theological sense of the word, a human being is not limited by his individual nature. He is not only a part of the whole, but potentially includes the whole, having in himself the whole of the earthly cosmos'.[21] To be in Christ brings to life this profound sense that man – truly perceived and truly perceiving – is both a part of the whole creation and contains the whole creation within himself.

It may be that the crucial words are those of St Paul: 'You are not your own'.[22] Indeed, such a state – the sovereign, independent, autonomous person – does not and cannot exist. It is only the deceit of sin which suggests that this is what we are. It is part of the liberating truth of the gospel to discover to whom we can and must belong. Thus it is that St Paul can say, 'If one member suffers, all suffer together; if one member is honoured, all rejoice together'.[23] This does not involve any loss of identity, but rather a discovery of our true identity as children of God, belonging to one another in Him. It is in the light of this conviction that eastern orthodox thought speaks of man as possessing one single nature in many human persons.[24]

The relationship of Christ to His body is unique, but the nature of His relationship is such that it invests each member of the body and his activity with a new significance. 'If Christ identifies Himself with each of His disciples, then there must be a sense in which each represents Christ to the others'.[25] The relationship between Christ and those who put their faith in Him brings a social dimension into atonement theology; but the emphasis upon our solidarity with each other does not necessarily take us back into an exclusively man-centred understanding of atonement. The transformation of the world which is the passion of the Holy Spirit involves the bringing in of the kingdom. The proclamation of the kingdom involves a personal call to repentance and faith; but the consequences of discipleship are personal and social. Athanasius spoke of the Wisdom of God harmonising all things – things earthly and things heavenly – so that He might make 'one world order in beauty and harmony'.[26] If all forms of life are bound up in one another, intimately and profoundly interconnected, then the consequences of this process of transformation which is God's continuing work of atonement must be personal and social, corporate and cosmic.

Beyond all these things lies some perception of the mystery of atonement. 'Seek for yourself, O man, seek for your true self. He who seeks shall find – but, marvel and joy, he will not find himself, he will find God, or if he find himself, he will find himself in God'.[27] This experience of finding ourselves in God, has been expressed in many ways. The writer of the First Letter of St John points beyond present experience to the final destiny: 'Beloved, we are God's children now; it does not yet appear what we shall be, but we know that when He appears we shall be like Him, for we shall see Him as He is.'[28] The hope that we shall be like Him goes far beyond a mere imitation or replication of Christ. It has been understood as a call to become Christ. 'Let us rejoice and give thanks. Not only are we become Christians but we are become Christ. . . . If He is the Head and we are the members, then together He and we are *the whole man*'.[29] To be in Christ is to live in the passion of the cross. To be in Christ is to be transformed by the power of the Holy Spirit. To be in Christ is to explore the mystery of atonement. It is life in God.

Baptism and eucharist portray and re-present the saving events of Christian faith. They are rites of renewal because they involve a participation in the pattern of life and death and life.

Connections were made at any early stage in the life of the church between the baptism of Jesus in the Jordan, the baptism of Jesus in His death, and the baptism of the Christian disciple.[30] The primary connection was between the death and resurrection of Jesus and the call to holiness of living. Baptism was not, therefore, merely initiation into the body of Christ, but into the new life where God reigns. It was because of its association with the death and resurrection of the Lord that baptism was significant both for the community and the individual.

The solidarity of Christian people in which all are one in Christ is made explicit in baptism.[31] The waters of baptism continue to have many associations, but the requirement that a man be born of water and the spirit speaks again of the corporate nature of the new life in Christ. Baptism is about participation in the divine life, but the gifts of the Spirit are corporate; that is to say, they are bestowed on individuals to empower for growth and for action in the church and in the world.

The eucharist is not merely a liturgical representation of the sacrifice of Christ. It is the means whereby all members of the body are able to make the sacrifice their own and become one with Christ in His self-offering. Frances Young insists that the sacrificial language that was used by the early church did not only speak of the response of the Christian community to the sacrifice of Christ; it told of a participation in the sacrifice.[32]

The understanding of the eucharist as a sacrifice is entirely appropriate on the basis of all that is known about the meaning of sacrifice and in the light of St Paul's account of the institution of the eucharist which relates the sacrifice of the eucharist to the story of the community. It takes it back to the events in which the community had its origins. It provides links for the community with its past and its future. It renews the life of the community. It is, therefore, an act of celebration, a sacrifice of praise and thanksgiving.

It is one of the great strengths of baptism and eucharist that through their use of water, bread and wine, the church is reminded of the power of symbols, connecting her own interior life with the drama of creation. If it is possible to look beyond the distinction between the sacred and the profane and see that all life is one, then baptism and eucharist become so much more than the cultic acts of a confessional church. They will serve that purpose, but the church herself will be caught up in 'the total reconciling activity of God. . . . God's eternal drama of sacrifice.'[33] And so the eucharistic liturgy has been described as 'an offering of the world to God by man . . . a movement from this world into the world to come.'[34] The whole race, the whole universe, is caught up in this offering, this coming to God.[35]

It is this understanding of the symbolism, the meaning and the power of baptism and eucharist that is captured in the prayer of Teilhard de Chardin. 'To the full extent of my power, because I am a priest, I wish from now on to be the first to become conscious of all that the world loves, pursues and suffers; I want to be the first to seek, to sympathise and to suffer; the first to open myself out and sacrifice myself – to become more widely human and more nobly of the earth than of the world's servants.'[36] Here is the prayer of the priest that he might participate in the passion of the world as it is caught up in the passion of the cross. Here is the sacrifice – the offering – of love that transforms the world.

It is in the life of prayer that these things can be explored. 'The glory of God is a man who is truly alive'.[37] It is in prayer that the extent of God's glory and the depths of life in Christ can be discovered. For the Christian, to pray is to enter into life in the mind and spirit of Jesus: that is to say, with complete openness to the God who is the centre and ground of being, and without knowing where it will lead. Prayer involves the discovery and the exploration of God and of ourselves. 'In prayer we discover what we already have. You start where you are and deepen what you already have, and you realise that you are already there. We already have everything, but we don't know it and we don't experience it. Everything has been given to us in Christ. All we need is to experience what we already possess'.[38]

The initiative in prayer remains with God. Prayer is His work in us. It is not we who pray to God. It is God who prays in us. This is the substance of St Paul's powerful picture of the Spirit coming to the aid of our weakness, pleading for God's own people in God's own way.[39] What God requires is the response of faith and love which sets the Spirit free.

Prayer presupposes an awareness of God, but it is not possible to pray without love. Prayer is bound, therefore, to ask these questions of a Christian disciple: Do you love? What do you love? How much do you love? 'Only the man who seeks everything in God prays to Him. . . . Only the man who seeks nothing in himself seeks everything in God'.[40] Prayer brings into play the mind and the heart, the instincts, the intuition and the will, the imagination and the feelings, the love and the laughter and the tears. But it is part of the meaning of prayer for this generation that people are feeling after patterns of prayer in which words matter far less and silence matters far more. It is part of the rediscovery of prayer that 'simply waiting for God in silence *is* prayer. Indeed it is the most profound form of prayer that man in his torn and suffering state can offer to God'.[41]

It is in silence that the rhythms of the Spirit's activity, the meaning of all that is happening around us, can be discerned. And the prayer of the Church is set within the continuing prayer of Christ who is the head of the body. Prayer is set, therefore, within the life of God Himself. It is within the context of the church's corporate life of prayer, the unceasing rhythm of eucharist and office, of contemplation and intercession, that the individual prays and finds that his prayers are taken up into a greater offering and a greater unity.

There are rare moments in the life of prayer when all self-awareness, all sense of time and place, are lost. It is then that the disciple is most conscious of the truth that prayer is something God does. True prayer must therefore have something of the character of God's self-emptying love. It cannot be otherwise. Contemplation and intercession both require the abandonment of self in God and the empathy of prayer that is content to enter into, stand with and offer the other. There is, of course, a conscious disposition, an attitude of mind, a self-offering, an act of will; and there is the knowledge that God alone knows how He will use our prayer.

Thomas Merton writes of the part that is played by the contemplative – unseen, unknowing. 'You just lie there, inert, helpless, alone, in the dark, and let yourself be crushed by the inscrutable tyranny of time. The plank bed becomes an altar and you lie there without trying to understand any longer in what sense you can be called a sacrifice. Outside in the world, where it is night, perhaps there is someone who suddenly sees that something he has done is horrible. He is most unexpectedly sorry and finds himself able to pray.'[42] There is an awareness here of the mysterious energies that are continuously at work sustaining and renewing life and in which all can participate through prayer. This is the contribution that our silent acts of prayer can make to God's work of atonement.

There is a connection between contemplation and intercession. The former is learning to be still with God and to be content with God and to be lost in God. The latter is learning to bring into our stillness with God that other person or situation for which we are compelled to pray. And in the quietness of intercessory prayer it is also possible to lose all awareness of self. Anthony Bloom reminds us that intercession comes from a Latin word which means taking a step that brings us to the centre of the conflict.[43] It is in intercession that we discover the empathy of prayer. It is not possible to pray for another person, for some situation of hope or despair, without entering the sorrow or the joy and making them our own. It is here that the meaning of the mystical body of Christ comes to life, because 'in the invisible world we are all most deeply interconnected. . . . What happens to us when we pray is happening for all men everywhere'.[44]

And yet there lies beyond the solidarity of prayer some glimpse of a deeper belonging. This was some small part of the experience of Jesus as he discovered that, 'I and the Father are one'.[45] It was not the relationship of the observer and the observed, the lover and the beloved. It went beyond the relationship of a son and a father except in so far as the Son was in the Father and the Father in the Son. Beyond all human analogies and distinctions, Jesus knew Himself to be at one with the Father who led him on to an ever deeper awareness and obedience.

Bloom records an episode from the life of Father Silouan, a Russian artisan who came to Mount Athos and was put in charge of one of the workshops where other young peasants from distant villages were indented for a year or two to raise a little money they could get in no other way. Father Silouan's custodianship of these men went far beyond a routine observance of their work. He tells how he prayed for one of the men, his young wife and their child; how the sense of the divine presence overtook him as he prayed even to the point where he lost sight of the man, the woman and the child for whom he was praying; but how he found himself praying for them, then, with the love of God and, drawn into the depths, discovered the divine love.[46] Here is a pattern of prayer – a quality of praying – that takes us into depths that remain unknown to most of us, and yet it displays marvellously the experience of being at one with each other and with God that is there within our reach in the life of prayer.

It is participation in the divine life that lies at the heart of our being in Christ. This encompasses the call to holiness, the rediscovery of our humanity and of our solidarity with each other, the exploration of the mystery of our atonement. Baptism, eucharist and prayer have their indispensable place; but a Christian spirituality is concerned with the whole of living. The early Greek concept of deification was given a new interpretation by Gregory of Nyssa who directed attention to participation not in the being but in the activity of God. 'To become God, then, is to act as God acts, in love, in poverty, in compassion'.[47]

Holiness requires contemplation and action. Some will be drawn more fully in one direction because of temperament, experience, the expectations and opportunities of circumstance, application. Both are fundamental to being in Christ and for most people the balance must be held if there is to be a personal at-one-ment and some part in the wider at-one-ment in which we are called to share – the transformation of the world through the passion of the Holy Spirit into the image of the Son of God. 'Action is charity looking outward to other men, and contemplation is charity drawn inward to its own divine source.'[48]

The compulsion is love and it comes from within through the patient working of the Holy Spirit. The tasks to which it leads will lie beyond ourselves. They will be determined by our life in the mystical body of Christ and by our life in the world. This is part of what it means to be called by the Spirit of God to become the sons of God.

A true understanding of atonement in the world enables us to see that God and my neighbour and myself are all bound up in one another. And it is not just a question of doing the will of God. Only, then, is man truly at one with God. 'To conform to the will of God is to contribute to the healing of the world; to depart from it is to add to the chain of evil which weighs upon us all'.[49]

It is part of the transforming work of the Holy Spirit that God can be seen in all the circumstances of life. Prayer deepens the awareness of all that God is doing in the world, the sense of responsibility because of our solidarity with all people, the moral sensitivities, and the divine imperative at work within us. Prayer leads to a new responsibility for the unacceptable parts of our world, the confusion, the pain, the self-destruction; and yet it transcends them.

It is Merton again who captures the extent to which we are all bound up in one another as we find our atonement or our lack of atonement in the world. 'Only when we see ourselves in our true human context, as members of a race which is intended to be one organism and "one body", will we begin to understand the positive importance not only of the successes but of the failures and accidents in our lives. My successes are not my own. The way to them was prepared by others. The fruit of my labours is not my own: for I am preparing the way and the achievements of another. Nor are my failures my own. They may spring from the failure of another, but they are also compensated for by another's achievement. Therefore the meaning of my life is not to be looked for merely in the sum total of my own achievements. It is seen only in the complete integration of my achievement and failures with the achievements and failures of my own generation, and society, and time. It is seen above all, in my integration in the mystery of Christ'.[50]

What is glimpsed here is an understanding of our atonement which comes out of a holistic approach to life, which sees the human race as one organism, and which looks beyond our integration with each other to our final integration in Christ when God's purposes for the whole creation will be fulfilled.

## Chapter 21

# All in All

The perception of all that God is doing in the world will be sharpened by the prayer which unites contemplation and action and which sets the raw material of experience within a wider vision. But, if it is true that the creation waits with eager longing for the revealing of the sons of God until the time when the creation itself will be set free from its bondage to decay,[1] the necessity that is placed upon the sons and daughters of God to discern the purposes of God and to work with them takes on a new imperative. If the created order is to be free, men and women must be free. If the created order is to be whole, men and women must be whole.

The experience of Jesus suggests that there are three essential ingredients – solitude, identification and suffering – if the pattern and the purpose of God's activity is to be seen and to be made our own.

It is an early Christian insight that a man is what he does with his silence.[2] The injunction of Jesus that those who pray should go into their room and shut the door and pray to our Father who is in secret[3] points towards a pattern of withdrawal that was fundamental to His discipleship. This dimension of solitude, of standing alone with God, is related by St Paul to the passion of the Lord. 'For you have died, and your life is hid with Christ in God'.[4]

Solitude is one of the ways in which there can be a discovery of God, our neighbour and our self. 'Not everyone can or should live as a hermit. But no Christian can do without an inner hermitage in which to meet his God'.[5] All who seek the truth will know something of the darkness and the light, the sorrow and the joy, of silent withdrawal. There is a handing over in the solitude of prayer when all conscious acts of affirmation, empathy, petition cease; and all is silence and waiting upon God. This is the way that leads to a new and deeper awareness. It sets us free for God and for other people. It makes it possible to live entirely in the present. It gives access to the hidden reserves of truth and love and power, to the energy of the cross.

It is in solitude that something can be learned of what it means to identify with the pain of the world. There are repeated references in the gospels to the compassion that Jesus felt for those who pressed upon Him, but no incident speaks more powerfully of His identification with the travail of the world than the picture of Jesus weeping over the city.[6] St Paul's word for the church at Corinth might almost have been written as a commentary upon that scene. 'I said before that you are in our hearts, to die together and to live together'.[7]

It is possible to see here the compassion which is born of an identification with His people and which is carried through to the point where the power of transforming love, the energy that redeems, can do its work. In silence we learn to share the conflicts of our world, the lost opportunities, the possibilities for change, the joys, the sorrows: to enter them, to make them our own. 'I wonder whether you realise a deep, great fact?' wrote Baron von Hugel, 'That souls – all humans souls – are deeply interconnected. That we cannot only pray for each other, but suffer for each other'.[8] Here is an insight into what it meant for Jesus and must therefore mean for His disciples to enter into life and to be at one with all around us.

One of the consequences of deep identification can be an intuitive awareness of the truth of a situation. An illustration of what this can mean in an extreme form could be taken from the personal experiences of Carl Gustav Jung. His repeated visions of great tides of blood in the years preceding the First World War defied all explanation, but with the outbreak of hostilities he experienced a great sense of relief because the war provided some kind of cosmic explanation.[9] It is a rare instance of a prophetic capacity to see beyond the appearance of events and discern the things that shall be. And yet behind these horrendous visions lay his early years in clinical practice in the Burgholzi, his conviction that there was something in the experience of derangement that was fundamental to the human condition, his total commitment to his work. It is a demonstration of that special kind of empathy, identification, participation, that makes it possible to go beyond the processes of rational thought and capture the inner meaning and the inevitability of the human drama.

The second consequence of deep identification can be healing for others, the possibility of new life. Contemporary history provides a helpful illustration. In 1932, while in prison, the Mahatma Ghandi fasted as a protest against the mistreatment by the Hindus of India's sixty million people who were judged to be untouchable. It is not possible to see this fast in isolation from the whole life of the man and all that he represented. There was an extraordinary response throughout the country and, although the fast could not break the curse of untouchability, it destroyed the public approval it had previously enjoyed. A deep identification with the needs of people – carried through at great personal cost – can lead to consequences that are ethical, personal and social.

But the pattern of Jesus suggests that solitude, identification *and suffering* are inescapable and inseparable. From different parts of the world and from different religious traditions, men have testified to the power of suffering. It was Ghandi's conviction that he would never know God if he did not wrestle with evil even to point where it might cost him his life.[10] It was Bonhoeffer's experience that personal suffering is a more effective means of exploring the world than personal good fortune.[11] This is no new discovery. St Paul rejoiced in his suffering that he might complete in his flesh what is lacking in Christ's affliction for the sake of His body, that is the church.[12] The writer of the First Letter of St Peter spoke of the divine approval that rests on the one who, mindful of God, endures pain whilst suffering unjustly.[13] It is impossible to evaluate the power – the creative energy – that belongs to those who suffer for the sake of a greater good.

Suffering is part of the story of our humanity. It is part of the mystery of our atonement.

And yet there is joy! Christianity belongs to this world. It means 'living unreservedly in life's duties, problems, successes and failures, experiences and perplexities. In doing so we throw ourselves completely into the arms of God, taking seriously, not our own sufferings, but those of God in the world – watching with Christ in Gethsemane'.[14] The Christian life is a journey into God. It encompasses the darkness and the light, the suffering, the gaiety, the silent offering of pain in prayer, the bubbling up of the human spirit. Its meaning is to be found in a cross. Its promise is that God shall be all in all.

This promise goes far beyond all our immediate preoccupations. Nothing less than a holistic theory of atonement with dimensions that are personal, social and cosmic will do justice to the immensity of all that is meant by God and to the comprehensive claims that are inseparable from the Christian revelation. The experience of life is invariably one of fragmentation. Men and women do not possess wholeness; and yet it is in the moments of self-abandonment in God, when all self-awareness, all striving and seeking, all thought and feeling are stilled, that there comes the mystical experience of being at one with the One who is the beginning and end of all life. Here is 'the hint half-guessed, the gift half-understood'.[15] It is the anticipation received in faith of the good things God has prepared for those who love Him.[16] It is to pass from life through death to life.

It is an essential part of this experience to find that, 'We are all one life in God'.[17] There is something here that goes beyond an awareness of our common humanity. Every one is so completely bound up in each other that thoughts, words, feelings, actions – for good or for ill – redound to our mutual advantage or disadvantage. 'The whole of the past is involved in every human situation. . . . We never know whose love, whose prayers, whose fidelity in similar stress to some idea of good, brought up the strength available to us to the amount sufficient. . . . And it may well be that evil forms a similar system that wrong choices, indulged glooms, relished hates all have a way of belonging, and together form a network of spreading malevolence. . . . We do not know what we are doing in the sense that we cannot know the whole tale which results'.[18] This does not remove from any one of us the responsibility for what we are and what we do. It is merely to recognise that we are all shaped by influences of which we are totally unaware; and, moreover, that we have the power to influence in ways that cannot be seen the manner in which the continuing drama of man's story, of God's creation, is to be unfolded.

An intriguing illustration of this truth is provided in the world of the natural sciences by the high-energy collisions of sub-atomic particles as a method by which these particles can be observed. The particles created in these collisions may live for less than one millionth of a second before they disintegrate into protons, neutrons and electrons; and yet these particles can be detected, their properties can be measured, and they can be made to leave tracks which can be photographed.[19] This is a helpful analogy of the way in which everyone influences for good or for ill the world around us. Each thought, each word, each feeling, each action might only live for an extremely short time. It will then disintegrate in the sense that it will cease to be conscious, audible, visible, tangible. But it continues to leave tracks in the whirlpool of life. Nothing can ever be the same again. This is the measure of our at-one-ness with each other. We are one humanity, one flesh, one creation.

The Elder in *The Brothers Karamazov* reminded the monks before his death that we are all responsible for all people and for all things on earth.[20] It is part of the experience of our oneness in Christ that we are all most deeply interconnected, 'that everybody is my neighbour and my neighbour is myself'.[21] And there is a dimension in our Christian faith which takes us beyond our solidarity with one another in time to our solidarity with one another in God for all eternity.

St Julian of Norwich spoke of God's desire for the salvation of all men: 'The same thirst and longing that He had upon the rood-tree – that same desire, longing and thirst (if I see it aright) was in Him from without beginning; He hath the same now and shall have, unto the time that the last soul to be saved shall have come up to His bliss'.[22] The conviction that God shall be all in all does not lead inevitably to a complacent and uncritical universalism. Mother Julian takes the cross back into the life of God. It was there from without beginning. She makes explicit the eternal sacrifice of suffering love. The pattern of life and death and life remains. Life does not necessarily lead through death to life. And yet, if we are all so deeply interconnected, it is difficult to imagine the accomplishment of God's purposes unless and until the whole creation rejoices in God and finds its fulfilment in Him. Within the imagery of Christian faith and mysticism, which speaks of the divine thirst, there is to be found the invitation to share in the passion of the Son of God, the eternal longing that God shall be all in all.[23]

This eschatological dimension takes on new meaning in the light of all that is known about creation. It is no longer sufficient to expound the conviction that the cross tests everything merely in terms of the redemption of humanity. Man's period of sovereignty on earth has been so short, his evolution as a species is so intimately bound up with the continuing evolution of the universe, the awareness of the essential unity of life is such, that nothing less than a cosmic understanding of the cross can claim to be credible. If all life is contained within God, then all life has meaning for God and is penetrated by His purposes of love.

The approach can only be tentative but what is being sought is no new and speculative theology. It is, rather, an attempt to enlarge the awareness of a dimension that has always been present in our faith but that calls today for a fuller explication. Angela of Foligno, the thirteenth century Italian mystic, spoke of the plenitude of God in which, comprehending the whole world, she could see nothing but the divine power and could only marvel that, 'The whole world is full of God'.[24] Nicholas of Cusa, the fifteenth century German mystic and philosopher, spoke of the enfolding and the unfolding of the whole creation in God: 'Divinity is in all things in such a way that all things are in Divinity'.[25] These insights find a fair parallel in the passionate plea of Father

Zossima in his Discourses to love the whole of God's creation in order to perceive the divine mystery in things.[26] The ancient tradition that the whole creation is destined to share in the glory of God commends itself to our world. Christian theology is required to recognise that, 'The power of the risen Christ extends to the universe itself. Everything in heaven and on earth is included and summed up in Christ'.[27]

This all-embracing Christian hope is grounded in the death and resurrection of Jesus. Hope is a gift of God – 'total, unexpected, incomprehensible, undeserved'[28]; but it is necessary to go down into nothingness to receive it. Hope that is seen is not hope,[29] and Thomas Merton goes beyond the words of St Paul to portray Christian hope as 'the acceptance of life in the midst of death, not because we have courage, or light, or wisdom to accept, but because by some miracle the God of life Himself accepts to live in us at the very moment when we descend into death'.[30] Christian hope is confidence in the power of God; but the power of God is the folly of the cross. The element of sacrifice remains.

The Christian understanding of atonement involves a participation in Christ's pattern of self-emptying love. It is 'a lifetime's death in love'[31] that provides the key to the universal *motif* of life and death and life. It will take a variety of forms. It can be encountered in the quiet perseverance of those who live with the disappointments and frustrations of human relationships; in the courage of those who face permanent disability or terminal illness with honesty and courage and are not destroyed by despair; in the countless deserts of the mind and of the spirit through which men and women are required to travel as part of their journey. These are some of the innumerable private descents into nothingness and death that are lived out every day, but they are not experienced in a vacuum. These things communicate themselves to those around. They are commonplace illustrations of the energy of truth and love and patience and endurance.

But the moment of *death* can also be the moment of new creation. From depths within ourselves, from depths within all that constitutes life and holds it in being, forces are released which make for life and not for death. The wholeness that God desires to accomplish for His creation encompasses the darkness and the destruction; but the power, the energy, of the new creation cannot be released without the sacrifice of the cross, the pattern of death and resurrection.

The possibilities that are contained within the Christian hope bring us back to the questions concerning the end of man. But to ask questions concerning the end of man is to ask questions concerning the end of all things. What, then, is our final atonement? Where does it all lead? What purpose is being served? Is there some vision that transcends the experience of fragmentation, disillusion and decay? Is there a plan for the fullness of time that all things – things in heaven and things on earth – shall be united in the incarnate Son of God? What does it mean that God will be all in all?

There are moments of insight and encounter; but there are also limits to all knowledge, to the truth of all experience. There is a desire to move, 'Into another intensity, For a further union, a deeper communion'.[32] The language of the poets and the experience of the mystics point towards a fulfilment in which all conflict and contradictions are resolved. 'There is something in the depths of our being that hungers for wholeness and finality'.[33] Is this life's mockery, its cruel act of self-deception? Or is it, perhaps, the clue to life's deepest meaning? The writings of the mystics speak of 'an overwhelming experience of unity as the *summum bonum* of existence'.[34] Christian hope, grounded in the death and resurrection of Jesus, looks towards a final act that gathers up all things in God and holds them in Him for all eternity.

The petition in Jesus' high priestly prayer is a reminder that it is in the unity of the divine life that our atonement is to be found. The early Greek fathers spoke of *theosis*, the deification or divinization of man. The idea has been interpreted in various ways. It speaks of the conviction that ultimately there is no life that is outside God. But man does not stand apart from the created order. Atonement is not achieved by some conscious attempt on man's part to imitate or reproduce the pattern of Christ's obedience. The patterns of interdependence and interaction persist. The elements of necessity and chance remain. The *motif* of life and death and life cannot

be removed. But new life is the gift of God who is continuously present – creating, redeeming, restoring, renewing. The
meaning of atonement is to have for ourselves no life, no
love, but the life and love of God. It is to live in the fullness
of the divine life in which God is all in all. Our eternity is the
discovery of God in His eternity. The vision that confronts
us is one of 'endless Godhead endlessly possessed'.[35] Man is
called to share in the vocation of the whole creation which
is to be possessed by God in glory.

# Notes

## PREFACE

1 Crux omnia probat. *Luther's Works*, Weimar Ausgabe V. 179. 31.
2 Colossians i 19–20.
3 F. R. Barry, *The Atonement*, Hodder and Stoughton 1968, p. 9.
4 1 Corinthians i 18–25.
5 F. C. Happold, *Religious Faith and Twentieth-Century Man*, DLT 1980, p. 162.
6 Dietrich Bonhoeffer, Letters and Papers from Prison, SCM Press 1971, p. 300.

## PART I: THE SEARCH FOR WHOLENESS

### Chapter 1: The Search for Wholeness
1 Ephesians i 10.
2 1 Corinthians xv 28.
3 Colossians i 19–20.
4 Crux omnia probat. *Luther's Works*, op. cit.
5 Doris Lessing, *The Golden Note-Book*, Grafton Books 1986, p. 239.
6 Ladislaus Boros, *Hidden God*, Search Press 1973, p. 70.
7 F. W. Dillistone, *The Christian Understanding of Atonement*, SCM Press 1984, p. 400.

### Chapter 2: The Living World
1 James Lovelock, *The Ages of Gaia*, OUP 1988.
2 John V. Taylor, *The Go-Between God*, SCM Press 1978, pp. 28–30.
3 J. Z. Young, *An Introduction to the Study of Man*, Clarendon Press 1971 p. 640.
4 Ibid, p. 115.
5 Ibid, pp. 640–1.
6 Peter L. Berger, *Invitation to Sociology*, Penguin Books 1971, p. 159.
7 Leo Tolstoy, *War and Peace*, Trans. by Rosemary Edmonds, Penguin Books 1986 p. 718.

8 Ibid, p. 717.
9 North-South: A Programme for Survival. *Report of the International Commission on International Development Issues*, Pan Books 1980, p. 33.
10 Ibid, pp. 10–11.
11 Ibid, p. 268.
12 Ibid, p. 268.
13 Lawrence Le Shan, *Holistic Health*, Turnstone Press 1984, p. 36.
14 Ibid, pp. 93–4.
15 Lawrence Le Shan, *You Can Fight for Your Life*, Turnstone Press 1984, p. 9.
16 Ibid, p. xv.
17 Fyodor Dostoyevsky, *The Brothers Karamazov*, Trans by David Magarshack, Penguin Books 1985, p. xxii.
18 Russell Ash, *The Impressionists*, Orbis Publishing 1980, p. 38.
19 Wilfred Owen, *War Poems and Others*, Chatto and Windus 1973, Appendix 1, p. 137.
20 Doris Lessing, *op. cit., p. 79*.
21 Peter Shaffer, *Amadeus*, Penguin Books 1985, p. 66.
22 Ibid.
23 Herbert Butterfield, *Christianity and History*, G. Bell 1949, p. 67.

### Chapter 3: A Holistic Theory

1 Martin Luther, *Heidelberg Disputation, Theses 19 and 20*. Cited by Walter von Loewenich, *Luther's Theology of the Cross*, Trans. by Herbert J. A. Bouman, Christian Journals Ltd Belfast 1976, p. 18.
2 Ludwig von Bertalanffy, *Chance or Law*. Essay published in *The Alphbach Symposium 1968: Beyond Reductionism – New Perspectives in the Life Sciences*, Ed. by Arthur Koestler and J. R. Smythie, Hutchinson 1969, p. 57.
3 1 Corinthians i 18–25.
4 Paul A. Weiss, *The Living System: Determinisn Stratified*. Essay published in *The Alphbach Symposium 1968*, op. cit., p. 5.
5 Ludwig von Bertalanffy, *op. cit.*, p. 57. von Bertalanffy cites here a public statement by the Premier of Alberta, Canada, in 1967.
6 L. Charles Birch, *Nature and God*, SCM Press 1965, p. 47.
7 W. H. Thorpe, *Man in Evolution*, Theology February 1969.
8 Fritjof Capra, *The Turning Point*, Fontana: Flamingo 1982. p. 293.
9 Ibid, p. 306.
10 Ibid, p. 313.
11 Barbara Ward and René Dubos, *Only One Earth*, Andre Deutsch 1972, p. 297.

**PART II: THE TASK OF THEOLOGY**

**Chapter 4: The Task of Theology**
1  A. R. Peacocke, *Creation and the World of Science*, Clarendon Press 1979, p. 48.
2  Meister Eckhart, *Sermon LXIX*.
3  Exodus iii 14.
4  Augustine of Hippo cited by F. C. Happold, *op. cit.*, page 125.
5  S. T. Achen, *Symbols Around Us*, Van Nostrand Reinhold Co. 1978, pp. 8 f.
6  Paul Tillich, *Systematic Theology*, Jas. Nisbet & Co. 1960, Vol. I, p. 196.
7  F. W. Dillistone, *The Power of Symbols*, SCM Press 1986, p. 135. Cites Karl Rahner, *Theological Investigations* 4, DLT 1966, pp. 235–252.
8  Keith Ward, *Holding Fast to God*, SPCK 1982, p. 19.
9  Karl Rahner, *Foundations of Christian Faith*, DLT 1978, p. 48.
10  Paul Tillich, *The Shaking of the Foundations (The Theologian)*, SCM Press 1957, p. 119.
11  Karl Barth, *Church Dogmatics*, T. & T. Clark 1975, Vol. I, Part 1, p. 14.
12  Romans i 19–20 (NEB).
13  Hebrews xi 6.
14  Hans Kung, *Does God Exist?*, Collins 1980, p. 508.
15  Acts xvii 28.
16  Cited by F. C. Happold, *Religious Faith and Twentieth Century Man*, DLT 1980, p. 170.
17  St Bonaventure, 1221–1274. Cited by H. A. Williams, *Poverty, Chastity and Obedience, (Oxford University Sermon)*, Mitchell Beazley 1975, p. 118.
18  H. A. Williams, *op. cit. (Hulsean Sermon)*, p. 24.
19  Ibid.
20  Ezekiel xliii 2.
21  2 Corinthians iv 6.
22  St John xv 5.
23  H. A. Williams, *op. cit. (Hulsean Sermon)*, p. 24.
24  Norman Pittenger, *After Death Life in God*, SCM Press 1980, p. 39.
25  1 Corinthians xii 12.
26  Norman Pittenger, *op. cit.*, p. 69.
27  Ibid. Also Norman Pittenger, *Picturing God*, SCM Press 1982, pp. 90–99.
28  Hosea xi 4.
29  Julian of Norwich, *Revelations of Divine Love*, Chapters, 52, 54, 58–64.
30  Hans Kung, *op. cit.*, pp. 632–3.
31  Karl Rahner, *Foundations of Christian Faith*, DLT 1978, p. 48.
32  Jean Daniélou, *God and Us*, Trans. by Walter Roberts, Mowbray & Co., 1957, p. 171.

**Chapter 5: God and Man**

1   Genesis i 31.
2   A. R. Peacocke, *op. cit.*, p. 142.
3   Grace M. Jantzen, *God's World God's Body*, DLT 1984, p. 130.
4   C. G. Jung, *Memories, Dreams, Reflections*, Fontana Paperbacks 1985, pp. 284–5.
5   Grace M. Jantzen, *op. cit.*, p. 151.
6   Genesis i 28.
7   Austin Farrer, *The Science of God*, Geoffrey Bles 1966, pp. 90–91.
8   *Ibid.*
9   Bede Griffiths, *The Marriage of East and West*, Collins 1982, p. 168.
10  Laurens van der Post, *Jung and the Story of Our Time*, Hogarth Press 1976, p. 237.
11  Ephesians iv 6.

**Chapter 6: God and Evil**

1   Isaiah xlv 7.
2   Jacob Boehme, *The Way to Christ*, Trans. by J. J. Stoudt, John M. Watkins 1953, p. 63.
3   Jacob Boehme, *op. cit.*, p. 163.
4   Ed. by Eleanor C. Rohrbach, *Jung's Contribution to Our Time: The Collected Papers of Eleanor Bertine*, C. G. Putnam 1967, pp. 54–5.
5   Laurens van der Post, *op. cit.*, p. 84.
6   Grace M. Jantzen, *op. cit.*, p. 92.
7   Ibid, p. 91.
8   Laurens van der Post, *op. cit.*, pp. 216–7.
9   Elie Weisel, *Night*, MacGibbon & Mee 1960, pp. 48–9.
10  Karl Barth, *Church Dogmatics*, T. & T. Clark 1961, Vol. III Part 3, pp. 289–368.
11  Ibid, p. 352.
12  Genesis i 2.
13  Karl Barth, *Church Dogmatics op. cit.*, Vol. III. Part 3, p. 352.
14  *Ibid.* p. 302.
15  Ibid, p. 366.
16  Paul Tillich, *Systematic Theology*, James Nisbet & Co. 1960, Vol. II, p. 52.
17  Ibid, p. 46.
18  Ibid, p. 50.
19  Ibid, p. 71.
20  Ibid, p. 49.
21  Ibid.
22  Ibid, p. 64.
23  Genesis iii v.
24  St Augustine of Hippo.
25  Elie Wiesel, *The Town Beyond the Wall*, p. 174. Cited by Kenneth Surin, *Theology and the Problem of Evil*, Basil Blackwell 1986, p. 120.
26  Kenneth Surin, *op. cit.*, p. 77.

## Chapter 7: The Triune God

1 T. F. Torrance, *The Trinitarian Faith*, T. &. T. Clark 1988, p. 202.
2 Ibid. pp. 311–12.
3 Jürgen Moltmann, *The Trinity and the Kingdom of God*, SCM Press 1981, p. 63.
4 Ed. by Gerald A. McCool, *A Rahner Reader*, DLT 1975, p. xxi.
5 Ibid, p. 193.
6 Karl Barth, *Dogmatics in Outline*, SCM Press 1985, p. 42.
7 Ibid.
8 Karl Barth, *Church Dogmatics*, T. & T. Clark 1988, Vol. IV, Part 1, p. 176.
9 Eberhard Jüngel, *The Doctrine of the Trinity*, Scottish Academic Press 1976, p. 108.
10 Ed. by Gerald A. McCool, *op. cit.*, p. 139.
11 Karl Barth, *Church Dogmatics*, T. & T. Clark 1988, Vol. IV, Part 1, p. 8.
12 Exodus xxxiii 20.
13 1 Timothy vi 16.
14 Jean Daniélou, *op. cit.*, p. 118.
15 Ephesians i 10.
16 Jan van Ruysbroeck, *The Spiritual Marriage*, III 1. 3. 4. Cited by David Brown, *The Divine Trinity*, Duckworth 1985, p. 209.

## PART III: THE MEANING OF SACRIFICE

## Chapter 8: Ancient Rites

1 René Girard, *Violence and the Sacred*, Trans. by Patrick Gregory, John Hopkins University Press 1972.
2 F. C. N. Hicks, *The Fullness of Sacrifice*, SPCK 1959, p. 28.
3 Lucien Lévy-Bruhl, *Primitive Mentality*, Trans. by Lilian A. Clare, George Allen & Unwin 1973, Translator's Note, p. v.
4 F. W. Dillistone, *Christianity and Symbolism*, SCM Press 1985, p. 224.
5 F. W. Dillistone, *The Christian Understanding of Atonement*, SCM Press 1984, p. 165.
6 F. W. Dillistone, *Christianity and Symbolism*, *op. cit.*, p. 224.
7 E. E. Evans-Pritchard, *Nuer Religion*, Clarendon Press 1970.
8 Ibid, p. 279.
9 Ibid, pp. 281–2.
10 G. Van Der Leeuw, *Religion in Essence and Manifestation*, Trans. by J. E. Turner, Peter Smith, Gloucester, Massachusets 1967, Vol. II, p. 351.
11 Ibid, Vol. II, p. 352.
12 H. Hubert and M. Mauss, *Sacrifice: Its Nature and Function*, Cohen and West 1964, p. 9. Cited by J. H. M. Beattie, *On Understanding Sacrifice*, Article published in *Sacrifice*, Ed. by M. F. C. Bourdillon and Meyer Fortes, Academic Press 1980, p. 34.

13  J. H. M. Beattie, *op. cit.*, p. 37.
14  H. Hubert and M. Mauss, *op. cit.*, p. 97.

### Chapter 9: Sacrifice in the Old Testament
1  F. C. N. Hicks, *op. cit.*, pp. 11–13.
2  Leviticus xvii 11.
3  H. H. Rowley, *From Moses to Qumran*, Lutterworth Press 1964, p. 91.
4  Isaiah xlii 1–4; xlix 1–6; l 4–9; lii 13 – liii 12.
5  H. H. Rowley, *op. cit.*, p. 105.

### Chapter 10: The Meaning of Sacrifice
1  Anthony Bloom, *God and Man*, DLT 1971, p. 68.
2  F. W. Dillistone, *The Power of Symbols*, SCM Press 1986, p. 69.
3  F. W. Dillistone, *The Christian Understanding of Atonement*, SCM Press 1984, p. 410.
4  Ibid, p. 411.
5  Ibid.
6  Ibid.
7  Robert J. Daly, *The Origins of the Christian Doctrine of Sacrifice*, DLT 1978, p. v.
8  Cyril C. Richardson, *The Eucharistic Sacrifice*, Anglican Theological Review, January 1950, pp. 57–8.

### PART IV: THE WORK OF CHRIST

### Chapter 11: The Work of Christ
1  2 Corinthians v 19.
2  Acts ii 22–4.
3  Acts iii 22.
4  Acts iii 13.
5  Acts iii 19, 25–6.
6  Acts ii 33.
7  Christopher Rowland, *Christian Origins*, SPCK 1985, p. 179.
8  Martin Hengel, *The Cross of the Son of God (The Son of God)*, SCM Press 1986, p. 55.
9  James Barr, *Some Thoughts on Narrative, Myth and Incarnation*. Essay published in *God Incarnate: Story and Belief*, Edited by A. E. Harvey, SPCK 1981. p. 22.
10  Colossians i 19.
11  Christopher Rowland, *op. cit.*, p. 174.
12  G. W. H. Lampe, *God As Spirit*, Clarendon Press 1977.
13  Ibid, p. 144.
14  Ibid, pp. 208–209.
15  Karl Barth, *Dogmatics in Outline*, SCM Press, 1988. p. 39.
16  Karl Barth, *Church Dogmatics*, T. & T. Clark 1958, Vol. III, Part 1, p. 318.

17 Ed. Gerald A. McCool, *A Rahner Reader*, DLT 1975, p. 167.
18 Hosea xi 1.
19 Hebrews i 2a.
20 St Irenaeus, *Adversus Haereses*, III.18.1.
21 Colossians i 19.
22 Ed. Gerald A. McCool, *op. cit.*, pp. 152–3.
23 Colossians i 17b.
24 Christopher Bryant, *Jung and the Christian Way*, DLT 1984, p. 84.
25 F. W. Dillistone, *The Power of Symbols*, SCM Press 1986, p. 180.
26 Ed. Gerald A. McCool, *op. cit.*, p. 169.
27 St Matthew iv 1–11; St Luke iv 1–13.
28 St Luke ix 57–62.
29 St Luke iv 33–4.
30 St Matthew xii 14, xxvi 3–4; St Mark xiv 1.
31 St Mark xiv 21.
32 St Luke ix 51.
33 C. F. D. Moule, *The Origin of Christology*, CUP 1977. p. 110.
34 St Matthew xxvi 39b.
35 Norman Pittenger, *Picturing God*, SCM Press 1982, p. 106.
36 Karl Rahner, *Jesus Christ and Christology*. Essay published in *A New Christology* by Karl Rahner and Wilhelm Thüsing, Burns and Oates 1980, p. 3.
37 A Monk of Marmion Abbey, *Becoming Christ*, Dimension Books: Denville New Jersey 1980, p. 19.
38 2 Corinthians v 14.
39 A Monk of Marmion Abbey, *op. cit.*, p. 12.
40 St John xii 24.
41 John Donne, *Sermon on Christmas Day* 1626.
42 Colossians iii 5–10.
43 Christopher Rowland, *op. cit.*, p. 114.
44 1 Corinthians xv 20b.
45 1 Corinthians xv 24–6.
46 1 Corinthians xv 28b.
47 Romans viii 2.
48 1 Corinthians vi 11.
49 Romans viii 14.
50 Leo the Great, *Serm.* 64.3. Cited by R.S. Franks, *The Work of Christ*, Thos. Nelson & Sons Ltd., 1962, p. 105.
51 Anthony Bloom, *op. cit.*, p. 52.
52 C. F. D. Moule, *op. cit.*, p. 122.

## Chapter 12: The Kingdom of God

1 St John xviii 37.
2 St John vi 38.
3 Frances Young, *A Cloud of Witnesses*. Essay published in *The Myth of God Incarnate*, Ed. by John Hick, SCM Press 1977, p. 15.
4 Christopher Rowland, *op. cit.*, p. 182.

5  Ibid, p. 186.
6  St John vi 27.
7  St Matthew xi 27.
8  Joachim Jeremias, *The Prayers of Jesus*, SCM Press 1967, pp. 96 f.
9  St John x 38.
10 St Matthew xix 17.
11 St John iii 11.
12 St Matthew x 37–9.
13 St Matthew xxiii 23.
14 St Luke ix 62.
15 St Matthew xii 28.
16 St Matthew iv 23.
17 St Matthew xi 3.
18 St Matthew xi 5.
19 Isaiah xxxv 2b but with reference to Isaiah xxxv 5–6.
20 St Luke xvii 21b.
21 St Matthew xxiv 14.
22 E. P. Sanders, *Jesus and Judaism*, SCM Press 1985, p. 113.
23 Wilhelm Thüsing, *New Testament Approaches to a Transcendental Christology*. Essay published in *A New Christology* by Karl Rahner and Wilhelm Thüsing, Burns and Oates 1980, p. 131.
24 Christopher Rowland, *op. cit.*, p. 113.
25 Martin Hengel, *Charismatic Leader*, Trans. by James C. Greig, T. & T. Clark 1981, pp. 20f.
26 A. E. Harvey, *Jesus and the Constraints of History*, Duckworth 1982, p. 64.
27 E. P. Sanders, *op. cit.*, p. 156.
28 St Luke xvi 16.
29 St Matthew xi 4–6.
30 E. P. Sanders, *op. cit.*, p. 307.
31 St Matthew xxvi 29.
32 E. P. Sanders, *op. cit.*, p. 22.
33 J. Neville Ward, *Friday Afternoon*, Epworth Press 1982, p. 11.

**Chapter 13: Jesus and His Passion**

1  Deuteronomy xxi 23.
2  St Mark xiv 8.
3  St Mark xiv 21a.
4  St Matthew xxvi 55–6.
5  St Matthew xvi 21.
6  St Luke xii 49–50.
7  St John xii 27–8.
8  St Mark x 45.
9  C. K. Barrett, *Jesus and the Gospel Tradition*, SPCK 1967, pp. 41–2.
10 C. K. Barrett, *The Background of Mark 10: 45*. Essay published in *New Testament Essays: Studies in Memory of T. W. Manson*, Ed. by A. J. B. Higgins, Manchester University Press 1959, p. 7.

11 St Luke xxii 37.
12 Vincent Taylor, *Jesus and His Sacrifice*, Macmillan 1939, p. 48.
13 Martin Hengel, *The Cross of the Son of God (The Atonement)*, SCM Press 1986, p. 247.
14 Ibid.
15 Christopher Rowland, *op. cit.*, pp.. 176–7.
16 St Mark xii 1–11; St Matthew xxi 33–43; St Luke xx 9–18.
17 St Luke xxiii 28.
18 St John xii 31–2.
19 St Mark viii 34–5.
20 St Mark x 39.
21 1 Corinthians xi 23–6.
22 Martin Hengel, *The Cross and the Son of God (Crucifixion)*, SCM Press 1986, p. 112.
23 C. G. Jung, *Memories, Dreams, Reflections*, Fontana 1985, p. 391.
24 C. F. D. Moule, *op. cit.*, p. 109.
25 St Luke ix 51.
26 Vincent Taylor, *op. cit.*, pp. 271–2.
27 W. H. Vanstone, *The Stature of Waiting*, DLT 1982, p. 31.
28 Ibid, p. 33.
29 St Matthew xxvi 39.
30 Jürgen Moltmann, *The Trinity and the Kingdom of God*, SCM Press 1981, p. 77.
31 St Mark xv 34.
32 Meister Eckhart, *Sermon, Qui audit me*.
33 Jürgen Moltmann, *The Crucified God*, SCM Press 1974, p. 151.
34 D. E. Nineham, *The Gospel of St Mark*, Penguin Books (The Pelican Gospel Commentaries) 1963, p. 428.
35 Elie Wiesel, *Night*, MacGibbon & Mee 1960. pp. 14–15.
36 St John xix 30 (NEB).
37 W. H. Vanstone, *op. cit.*, p. 85–6.
38 Ibid, p. 94.
39 Ibid, p. 95.
40 Austin Farrer, *op. cit.*, p. 19.

## PART V: THEORIES OF ATONEMENT

### Chapter 14: The Evidence of Scripture
1 Ignatius of Antioch, *To the Ephesians 19. 1.*
2 Ephesians i 10.
3 1 Corinthians i 23–4.
4 1 Corinthians xv 3–5.
5 Acts iv 33.
6 1 Peter i 3–5.
7 Christopher Rowland, *op. cit.*, p. 189.
8 Romans viii 22.

9 Frances Young, *Can These Dry Bones Live?*, SCM Press 1982, p. 53.
10 Christopher Rowland, *op. cit.*, p. 208.
11 Acts x 38–42.
12 Martin Hengel, *The Cross of the Son of God (Crucifixion)*, SCM Press 1986, p. 181.
13 Romans viii 32.
14 Martin Hengel, *The Cross of the Son of God (Crucifixion)*, *op cit.*, p. 181.
15 Galatians i 3–4.
16 2 Corinthians i 20.
17 Martin Hengel, *The Cross of the Son of God (Atonement)*, SCM Press 1986, p. 248.
18 Ibid.
19 John Downing, *Jesus and Martyrdom*, Journal of Theological Studies, Vol. xxiv (1963), p. 284.
20 1 Peter ii 24.
21 Hebrews ii 9.
22 Romans v 8.
23 2 Corinthians v 14–15.
24 Galatians ii 20.
25 Karl Barth, *Dogmatics in Outline*, SCM Press 1985, p. 107.
26 Robert J. Daly, *op. cit.*, p. 34.
27 2 Corinthians v 21.
28 R. S. Franks, *The Work of Christ*, Thos. Nelson & Sons 1962, p. 584.
29 St Mark x 45.
30 St John i 29.
31 1 Corinthians v 7b.
32 Ephesians v 2.
33 1 Peter i 19.
34 Hebrews xiii 11–12.
35 Philippians ii 8.
36 Hebrews x 12.
37 1 Peter iii 18.
38 Frances Young, *op. cit.*, p. 72.
39 Romans xii 1.
40 Romans iii 24–5.
41 1 John ii 2.
42 Frances Young, *Sacrifice and the Death of Christ*, SCM Press 1975, p. 71.
43 St John xv 13.
44 Galatians v 1.
45 Romans v 18–19.
46 F. W. Dillistone, *The Christian Understanding of Atonement*, SCM Press 1984, p. 177.
47 Romans vii 12.
48 Romans vii 10.

49 Romans i 18.
50 Galatians iii 13.
51 Anthony Bloom, *op. cit* p. 53.
52 Romans iii 9.
53 Romans iii 23.
54 C. H. Dodd, *Epistle to Romans*, Fontana (Moffatt Commentary) 1960 pp. 149–150.
55 Frances Young, *Can These Dry Bones Live?*, SCM Press 1982, p. 70.
56 Galatians ii 16.
57 Romans v 1–2.
58 Acts ii 38.
59 Colossians iii 3.
60 Ephesians iv 13.

## Chapter 15: Theories of Atonement

1 Irenaeus, c. 130 – c. 200, Bishop of Lyons.
2 Clement of Alexandria, c. 150 – c. 215.
3 Origen, c. 185 – c. 254.
4 Athanasius, c. 296–373, Bishop of Alexandria.
5 Gregory of Nazianzus, 329–389, Bishop of Constantinople.
6 Gregory of Nyssa, c. 330 – c. 395, Bishop of Nyssa.
7 Origen, *Contra Celsum i 31*. Cited by Frances Young, *Sacrifice and the Death of Christ*, SCM Press 1975, p. 79.
8 Frances Young, *Sacrifice and the Death of Christ*, SCM Press, 1975, p. 80.
9 Hilary, c. 315–367, Bishop of Poitiers.
10 Ambrose, c. 339–397, Bishop of Milan.
11 Tertullian, c. 160 – c. 220.
12 Augustine, 354–430, Bishop of Hippo.
13 J. N. D. Kelly, *Early Christian Doctrines*, A. & C. Black 1965, p. 391.
14 Anselm, c. 1033–1109, Archbishop of Canterbury.
15 R. W. Southern, *St Anselm and His Biographer*, CUP 1963. pp. 82–88.
16 O. C. Quick, *The Gospel of the New World*, Nisbet & Co 1944, p. 75.
17 R. W. Southern, *op. cit.*, p. 96.
18 Abelard. 1079–1142.
19 Richard E. Weingart, *The Logic of Divine Love*, Clarendon Press 1970.
20 R. W. Southern, *op. cit.*, pp. 92–3.
21 Richard E. Weingart, *op. cit.*, pp. 92–3.
22 Richard E. Weingart, *op. cit.*, p. 131.
23 Romans v 8.
24 O. C. Quick, *op. cit* pp. 89–90.
25 Martin Luther, *Schmalkald Articles, Part II*. Cited by R. S. Franks, *op. cit.*, p. 286.
26 Martin Luther, *Lectures on Galatians iii 13*. Luther's Works, Vol. 26, Lectures on Galatians, Chapters 1–4, Ed. by Jaroslov Pelika, Concordia Publishing House: St Louis 1963.
27 Martin Luther, 1483–1546.

28 Hastings Rashdall, *The Idea of Atonement in Christian Theology*, Macmillan & Co. 1919, p. 398.
29 Martin Luther, *In Gal. xvi 16*. Cited by Hastings Rashdall, *op. cit.*, p. 407.
30 John Calvin, 1509–1564.
31 R. S. Franks, *op. cit.*, p. 342.
32 John Calvin, *Institutes of the Christian Religion II. 21. 7*. F. R. Barry, *The Atonement*, Hodder & Stoughton 1968, p. 158.
33 Hebrews ix 22.
34 John Calvin, *Institutes of the Christian Religion II. 16. 10*. The Library of Christian Classics, Vol. XX, Ed. by John T. McNeil, SCM Press 1960, pp. 515–6.
35 Hastings Rashdall, *op. cit.*, p. 416.
36 Friedrich Schleiermacher, 1768–1834.
37 Albrecht Ritschl, 1822–1889.
38 John McLeod Campbell, 1800–1872.
39 John McLeod Campbell, *The Nature of the Atonement*, James Clarke & Co 1959, p. li.
40 R. C. Moberly, 1845–1903.
41 R. C. Moberly, *Atonement and Personality*, John Murray 1917, p. xiii.
42 Hastings Rashdall, 1858–1924.
43 R. S. Franks, 1871–1964.
44 Hastings Rashdall, *op. cit.*, pp 449–450.
45 R. S. Franks, *The Atonement*, OUP 1934; p. 172.
46 Gustaf Aulén, 1879–1978.
47 John of Damascus, c. 675 – c. 749.
48 Gustaf Aulén, *Christus Victor*, Trans. by A. G. Hebert, SPCK 1961, p. 59.
49 Ibid, pp. 123–9.
50 Ibid, pp. 152–6.
51 Gustavo Gutierrez, *A Theology of Liberation*, SCM Press 1974.
52 Ibid, p. 176.
53 Ibid.
54 Ibid, p. 159.
55 Ibid, p. 151.

**Chapter 16: Faith and Culture**
1 *The Catechetical Oration of St Gregory of Nyssa*. Trans. by J. H. Strawley. SPCK 1917, p.73.
2 Abelard, *Prob Heloissae VI 686 b*. Cited by Richard E. Weingart, *op. cit.*, p. 121.
3 Abelard, *Expos. in Epist. ad Rom ii 3*. Cited by Richard E. Weingart, *op. cit.*, p. 94.
4 R. W. Southern, *op. cit.*, p. 97.
5 Desiderius Erasmus, c. 1466–1536.
6 Erik Erikson, *Young Man Luther*, Faber & Faber 1958. p. 244.
7 Gustavo Gutierrez, *op. cit.*, p. 205.

8 O. C. Quick, *The Christian Sacraments*, Nisbet & Co. 1927, pp. 84–5.

## PART VI: THE MYSTERY OF ATONEMENT

### Chapter 17: The Mystery of Atonement

1 T. S. Eliot, *The Four Quartets (Burnt Norton)*.
2 Job xix 24.
3 Karl Barth, *Church Dogmatics*, T. & T. Clark 1961, Vol III, Part 3 pp. 289–368.
4 Paul Tillich, *Systematic Theology*, James Nisbet & Co 1960, Vol. II, p. 49.
5 Philippians ii 10–11.
6 1 Corinthians xv 28.
7 Sebastian Moore, *The Crucified Is No Stranger*, DLT 1977, p. 33.
8 Elizabeth R. Moberly, *Suffering, Innocent and Guilty*, SPCK 1978, p. 104.
9 Genesis iii 5.
10 H. R. Mackintosh, *The Christian Experience of Forgiveness*, Nisbet & Co 1927, p. 32.
11 J. Neville Ward, *op. cit*, p. 25.
12 Martin Jarrett-Kerr, *The Hope of Glory*, SCM Press 1952, p. 47.
13 F. C. N. Hicks, *op. cit.*, pp. 11–13.
14 St John xvii 24.
15 St John iii 16.
16 St John xiii 1.
17 1 John iii 16.
18 1 John iii 14.
19 Romans viii 38–9.
20 Ed. by Fritz A. Rothschild, *Between God and Man: An Interpretation of Judaism: From The Writings of Abraham Heschel*, Harper Bros 1959, pp. 116–124.
21 Nicholas Berdyaev, *The Meaning of History*, Goeffrey Bles 1936, pp. 45, 48, 55.
22 Kazok Kitamori, *Theology of the Pain of God*, SCM Press 1966, p. 71.
23 Miguel de Unamuno, *The Tragic Sense of Life in Men and Nations*, Routledge and Kegan Paul 1972, Vol. 4, p. 227.
24 Jürgen Moltmann, *The Crucified God*, SCM Press 1974, p. 246.
25 Bertrand Brasnett, *The Suffering of the Impassible God*, SPCK 1928, p. 11.
26 Abelard, *Prob. Heloissae VI 686b*. Cited by Richard E. Weingart, *op. cit.*, p. 121.
27 O. C. Quick, *The Gospel of the New World*, Nisbet & Co., 1944, p. 117.
28 St John xii 31.
29 Karl Barth, *Dogmatics in Outline*, SCM Press 1985, p. 135.

30 Wolfhart Pannenberg, *Future and Unity*. Essay published in *Hope and the Future of Man*, Ed. by Ewart H. Cousins, Garnstone Press 1973, p. 63.
31 H. R. Mackintosh, *op. cit.*, p. 187.
32 Jürgen Moltmann, *Creation and Redemption*. Essay published in *Creation, Christ and Culture: Studies in Honour of T. F. Torrance*, Ed. by Richard W. A. McKinney, T. & T. Clark 1976, p. 120.
33 Ibid, p. 128.
34 Ibid, p. 123.
35 Martin Jarrett-Kerr, *op. cit.*, p. 71.
36 D. M. MacKinnon, *The Relation of the Doctrines of the Incarnation and the Trinity*. Essay published in *Creation, Christ and Culture: Studies in Honour of T. F. Torrance, op. cit.*, p. 99.

## Chapter 18: The Sacrifice of God

1 Revelation xiii 8.
2 H. Bushnell, *The Vicarious Sacrifice*, Alexander Strahan 1866, p. 35.
3 Edith Sitwell, *Still Falls the Rain*.
4 C. F. D. Moule, *The Sacrifice of Christ*, Hodder & Stoughton 1956, p. 28.
5 Elie Wiesel, *Night*, MacGibbon & Mee 1960, pp. 82–3.
6 Jürgen Moltmann, *The Crucified God*, SCM Press 1974, pp. 273–4. Dorothy Soelle, *Suffering*, DLT 1975, p. 145.
7 H. H. Rowley, *op. cit.*, p. 182.
8 Frances Young, *Can These Dry Bones Live?*, SCM Press 1982, pp. 58–9.
9 1 Corinthians xv 36–7.
10 St John xii 24.
11 J. C. Smuts, *Holism and Evolution*, Victor Gollancz 1926, p. 82.
12 Richard Dawkins, *The Selfish Gene*, OUP 1976, pp. 6–7.
13 Ibid.
14 Christopher Bryant, *Jung and the Christian Way*, DLT 1983, p. 41.
15 Paul Tillich, *The Shaking of the Foundations (Escape from God)*, SCM Press 1957, p. 46.
16 Jürgen Moltmann, *The Crucified God, op. cit.* pp. 192–3.
17 St Matthew xxvii 45; St Mark xv 33; St Luke xxiii 44.
18 *Um Mitternacht*, A Song written by Mahler to the words of Friedrich Ruckert.

## Chapter 19: The Energy of the Cross

1 Fritjof Capra, *The Tao of Physics*, Fontana: Flamingo 1983, p. 11.
2 Peter L. Berger, *op. cit.*, p. 124.
3 Ibid.
4 C. G. Jung, *op. cit.*, p. 234.
5 Laurens van der Post, *op. cit.*, Hogarth Press 1976, pp. 118–9.
6 Ibid.
7 Ibid.

8 Paul Tillich, *The Shaking of the Foundations (Escape from God)*, SCM Press 1957, p. 46.
9 Christopher Bryant, *op. cit.*, p. 41.
10 J. Neville Ward, *op. cit* p. 25.
11 Rupert Sheldrake, *The Rebirth of Nature*, Century 1990.
12 Ibid. p. 80.
13 Ibid. p. 88.
14 Christopher Bryant, *op. cit.*, p. 84.
15 St John xx 19–22.
16 Laurens van der Post, *The Lost World of the Kalahari*, Penguin Books 1985, p. 171.
17 B. F. Westcott, *The Victory of the Cross*, Macmillan & Co 1888.
18 Ibid, p. 11.
19 Ibid, p. 21.
20 Bede Griffiths, *op. cit.*, p. 188.
21 Ed. by Louis Fischer, *The Essential Gandhi, An Anthology. His Life, Work and Ideas*, New York: Vintage Books 1962, p. 193.
22 B. F. Westcott, *op. cit.*, p. 85.
23 F. W. Dillistone, *The Christian Understanding of Atonement*, SCM Press 1984, p. 399.
24 Ed. by Hugh Montefiore, *Man and Nature*, Collins 1975, pp. 36.
25 F. W. Dillistone, *The Christian Understanding of Atonement*, *op. cit.*, p. 246.

## PART VII: LIFE IN GOD

### Chapter 20: Life in God

1 Vladimir Lossky, *The Mystical Theology of the Eastern Church*, James Clarke & Co., 1957, p. 39.
2 Ed. by Gerald A. McCool, *op. cit.*, p. 196.
3 Ibid.
4 Georges Bernanos, *The Diary of a Country Priest*, Trans. by Pamela Morris, Religious Book Club, p. 317.
5 Karl Barth, *Church Dogmatics*, T. & T. Clark 1975, Vol. I. Part 1. p. 466.
6 Ibid, p. 458.
7 Bede Griffiths, *op. cit.*, p. 96.
8 Fritjof Capra, *The Tao of Physics*, Fontana:Flamingo 1983, p. 30.
9 Bede Griffiths, *op. cit.*, p. 100.
10 Ibid. (2 Corinthians iii 18.)
11 Bede Griffiths, *op. cit.*, p. 93. Cites St Augustine of Hippo – Unus Christus amans seipsum.
12 Romans xii 5.
13 Vladimir Lossky *In the Image and Likeness of God*, Mowbray 1974, pp. 179–180.
14 Emile Mersch, *The Whole Christ*, Denis Dobson 1936, p. 105.

15  Ibid, p. 124.
16  Ephesians iv 13b.
17  Galatians v 24.
18  Galatians v 22–3.
19  St John xv 10.
20  Galatians ii 20.
21  Vladimir Lossky, *In the Image and Likeness of God, op. cit.* p. 107.
22  1 Corinthians vi 19b.
23  1 Corinthians xii 26.
24  H. A. Williams, *The Joy of God*, Mitchell Beazley 1975, p. 71.
25  L. S. Thornton, *The Common Life in the Body of Christ*, Dacre Press 1963, p. 40.
26  St Athanasius, *Oratio Contra Gentes* 42. Cited by Emile Mersch. *op. cit.*, p. 264.
27  Augustine, *Confessions*.
28  1 John iii 2.
29  Emile Mersche, *op. cit.*, p. viii.
30  W. F. Flemington, *The New Testament doctrine of Baptism*, SPCK 1948, pp. 115–127. O. Cullmann, *Baptism in the New Testament*, SCM Press 1950, p. 15.
31  Galatians iii 27–8.
32  Frances Young, *Sacrifice and the Death of Christ*, SCM Press 1975, pp. 96–7.
33  F. W. Dillistone, *The Christian Understanding of Atonement*, SCM Press 1984, p. 146.
34  A. M. Allchin, *The Theology of Nature in the Eastern Fathers and Among Anglican Theologians.*   Essay published in *Man and Nature*, Ed. by Hugh Montefiore, Collins 1975, p. 148.
35  Ibid.
36  Teilhard de Chardin, *Le Prêtre*. Cited by Eric James, *Odd Man Out?* Hodder & Stoughton 1962, p. 45.
37  Irenaeus, *Against Heresies*, I.6.2..
38  Ed. by Patrick Hart, *Thomas Merton: A Monk: A Monastic Tribute*, Hodder and Stoughton 1974, p. 80.
39  Romans viii 26–7.
40  Karl Barth, *Church Dogmatics*, T & T Clark, 1975, Vol.I Part 1. p. 465.
41  Ladislaus Boros, *The Cosmic Christ*, Trans. by David Smith, Search Press 1975, pp. 52–3.
42  Thomas Merton, *The Sign of Jonas*, Hollis & Carter, 1953, p. 41.
43  Anthony Bloom, *God and Man*, DLT 1971, p. 44.
44  H. A. Williams, *Becoming What I Am*, DLT 1977, p. 47.
45  St John x 30.
46  Anthony Bloom, *School for Prayer*, DLT 1970, pp. 75.
47  Rowan Williams, *The Wound of Knowledge*, DLT 1979, pp. 53–4.
48  Thomas Merton, *No Man Is An Island*, Harcourt Brace & Co 1955, p. 70.

49 Paul Tournier, *A Doctor's Casebook*, SCM Press 1954, p. 227.
50 Thomas Merton, *No Man Is An Island*, op. cit. pp. xxi-xxii.

## Chapter 21: All in All

1 Romans viii 19–21.
2 Mother Mary Clare, *Encountering the Depths*, DLT 1981, p. 20.
3 St Matthew vi 6a.
4 Colossians iii 3.
5 A Monk, *The Hermitage Within*, DLT 1977.
6 St Luke xix 41–4.
7 2 Corinthians vii 3.
8 Baron von Hugel, *Letters to a Niece*, J. M. Dent & Sons 1928, p. 25.
9 Laurens van der Post, *Jung and the Story of Our Time*, Hogarth Press 1976, p. 156.
10 Ed. Louis Fischer, *op. cit.*, p. 228.
11 Dietrich Bonhoeffer, *op. cit.*, p. 17.
12 Colossians i 24.
13 1 Peter ii 19.
14 Dietrich Bonhoeffer, *op. cit.*, p. 370.
15 T. S. Eliot, *Four Quartets (The Dry Salvages)*.
16 1 Corinthians ii 9.
17 Jan van Ruysbroeck, *The Twelve Beguines*, IV. 30. Cited by Eric Colledge in his Preface to *The Spiritual Espousals of Ruysbroeck*, Faber & Faber 1952, pp 17–18.
18 J. Neville Ward, *op. cit.*, p. 17.
19 Fritjof Capra, *The Tao of Physics*, Fontana: Flamingo 1983, p. 90.
20 Fyodor Dostoyevsky, *op. cit.*, p. 190.
21 H. A. Williams, *Becoming What I Am*, DLT 1977, p. 11.
22 Julian of Norwich, *Revelations of Divine Love*, Chapter 31.
23 1 Corinthians xv 28.
24 Angela of Foligno, c. 1248–1309. Cited by F. C. Happold, *op. cit.*, p. 131.
25 Nicholas of Cusa, cited by M. Fox, *The Coming of the Cosmic Christ*, Harper & Row 1988, p. 126.
26 Fyodor Dostoyevsky, *op. cit.*, p. 375.
27 Ladislaus Boros, *The Cosmic Christ*, Trans. by David Smith, Seurde Press 1975, p. 83.
28 Thomas Merton, *The New Man*, Burns & Oates 1961, p. 2.
29 Romans viii 24.
30 Thomas Merton, *The New Man*, op. cit., pp. 2–3.
31 T. S. Eliot, *Four Quartets (The Dry Salvages)*.
32 T. S. Eliot, *Four Quartets (East Coker)*.
33 Thomas Merton, *No Man Is An Island*, Harcourt Brace & Co. 1955, p. 124.
34 Jacob Boehme, *op. cit.*, p. xxxviii.
35 Austin Farrer, *The End of Man*, SPCK 1973, p. 4.

# Bibliography

S. T. Achen, *Symbols Around Us*, Van Nostrand Reinhold Co 1978.
Augustine, *Confessions*.
Gustaf Aulén, *Christus Victor*, SPCK 1961.
J. A. Baker, *The Foolishness of God*, DLT 1970.
C. K. Barrett, *The Background of Mark 10.45*, Essay in *New Testament Essays: Studies in Memory of T. W. Manson*, Ed. by A. J. B. Higgins, Manchester University Press 1959.
C. K. Barrett, *Jesus and the Gospel Tradition*, SPCK 1967.
F. R. Barry, *The Atonement*, Hodder and Stoughton 1968.
Karl Barth, *Church Dogmatics*, T. &. T. Clark.
Karl Barth, *Dogmatics in Outline*, SCM Press 1985.
Richard Bauckham, *Only the Suffering God Can Help: Divine Passibility in Modern Theology*, Themelios, Vol. 9 (1984).
Peter L. Berger, *Invitation to Sociology*, Penguin Books 1971.
L. Charles Birch, *Nature and God*, SCM Press 1965.
Anthony Bloom, *God and Man*, DLT 1971.
Jacob Boehme, *The Way to Christ*, Trans. by J. J. Stoudt, John M. Watkins 1953.
Dietrich Bonhoeffer, *The Cost of Discipleship*, SCM Press 1959.
Dietrich Bonhoeffer, *Letters and Papers from Prison*, SCM Press 1971.
Ladislaus Boros, *Hidden God*, Trans. by Erica Young, Search Press 1973.
Ladislaus Boros, *The Cosmic Christ*, Trans. by David Smith, Search Press 1975.
Ed. by M. F. C. Bourdillon and Meyer Fortes, *Sacrifice*, Academic Press 1980.
David Brown, *The Divine Trinity*, Duckworth 1985.
Ed. by D. Mackenzie Brown, *Ultimate Concern: Tillich in Dialogue*, SCM Press 1965.
Christopher Bryant, *Jung and the Christian Way*, DLT 1984.
J. MacLeod Campbell, *The Nature of the Atonement*, James Clarke & Co 1959.
Fritjof Capra, *The Turning Point*, Fontana: Flamingo 1982.
Fritjof Capra, *The Tao of Physics*, Fontana: Flamingo 1983.
George Carey, *The Gate of Glory*, Hodder and Stoughton 1986.
Gilbert Cope, *Symbolism in the Bible and the Church*, SCM Press 1959.
Robert J. Daly, *The Origins of the Christian Doctrine of Sacrifice*, DLT 1978.

Jean Daniélou, *God and Us*, Trans. by Walter Roberts, Mowbray & Co 1957.

F. W. Dillistone, *Myth and Symbol*, SPCK 1966.

F. W. Dillistone, *The Christian Understanding of Atonement*, SCM Press 1984.

F. W. Dillistone, *Christianity and Symbolism*, SCM Press 1985.

F. W. Dillistone, *The Power of Symbols*, SCM Press 1986.

Fyodor Dostoyevsky, *The Brothers Karamazov*, Penguin Books 1985.

John Downing, *Jesus and Martyrdom*, Journal of Theological Studies, Vol. xxiv (1963).

T. S. Eliot, *The Four Quartets*, Faber & Faber 1969.

Charles Elliott, *Praying the Kingdom*, DLT 1985.

E. E. Evans-Pritchard, *Nuer Religion*, Clarendon Press 1970.

Austin Farrer, *The End of Man*, SPCK 1973.

Austin Farrer, *The Glass of Vision*, Dacre Press 1958.

Thomas Fawcett, *The Symbolic Language of Religion*, SCM Press 1970.

Ed. by Louis Fischer, *The Essential Gandhi: An Anthology: His Life, Work and Ideas*, Vintage Books, New York, 1962.

P. T. Forsyth, *The Cruciality of the Cross*, Independent Press 1948.

R. S. Franks, *The Work of Christ*, Thos. Nelson & Son Ltd 1962.

S. C. Gayford, *Sacrifice and Priesthood*, Methuen & Co 1953.

René Girard, *Violence and the Sacred*, Trans. by Patrick Gregory, John Hopkins University Press 1972.

George Buchanan Gray, *Sacrifice in the Old Testament*, Clarendon Press 1925.

Bede Griffiths, *The Marriage of East and West*, Collins 1982.

Gustavo Gutierrez, *A Theology of Liberation*, SCM Press 1974.

F. C. Happold, *The Journey Inwards*, DLT 1976.

F. C. Happold, *Religious Faith and Twentieth Century Man*, DLT 1980.

Ed. by Patrick Hart, *Thomas Merton: Monk: A Monastic Tribute*, Hodder and Stoughton 1974.

Ed. by A. E. Harvey, *God Incarnate: Story and Belief*, SPCK 1981.

B. L. Hebblethwaite, *The Problems of Theology*, CUP 1980.

Martin Hengel, *The Cross of the Son of God (The Son of God, Crucifixion, Atonement)*, SCM Press 1986.

Abraham Heschel, *What Is Man?*, OUP 1966.

Ed. by John Hick, *The Myth of God Incarnate*, SCM Press 1977.

F. C. N. Hicks, *The Fullness of Sacrifice*, SPCK 1959.

H. Hubert and M. Mauss, *Sacrifice: Its Nature and Function*, Cohen and West 1964.

E. O. James, *Origins of Sacrifice*, John Murray 1933.

E. O. James, *Sacrifice and Sacrament*, Thames & Hudson 1962.

Grace M. Jantzen, *God's World, God's Body*, DLT 1984.

Martin Jarrett-Kerr, *The Hope of Glory*, SCM Press 1952.

C. G. Jung, *Memories, Dreams, Reflections*, Fontana 1985.

Eberhard Jüngel, *The Doctrine of the Trinity*, Scottish Academic Press 1976.

J. N. D. Kelly, *Early Christian Doctrines*, A. & C. Black 1965.

Kazok Kitamori, *Theology of the Pain of God*, SCM Press 1966.

Hans Kung, *Does God Exist?*, Collins 1980.

G. W. H. Lampe, *God As Spirit*, Clarendon Press 1977.

Doris Lessing, *The Golden Note-Book*, Grafton Books 1986.

Lawrence Le Shan, *Holistic Health*, Turnstone Press 1984.

Lawrence Le Shan, *You Can Fight For Your Life*, Thorsons Publishers 1984.

Vladimir Lossky, *In the Image and Likeness of God*, Mowbrays 1974.

James Lovelock, *The Ages of Gaia*, OUP 1988.

Ed. by Gerald A. McCool, *A Rahner Reader*, DLT 1975.

Alister McGrath, *The Enigma of the Cross*, Hodder and Stoughton 1987.

D. M. MacKinnon, *Subjective and Objective Conceptions of Atonement*, Essay in *Prospect for Theology: Essays in Honour of H. H. Farmer*, Ed. by F. G. Healey, Jas. Nisbet & Co 1966.

D. M. MacKinnon, *The Relation of the Doctrines of the Incarnation and the Trinity*. Essay in *Creation, Christ and Culture: Studies in Honour of T. F. Torrance*, Ed. by Richard W. A. McKinney, T. & T. Clark 1976.

H. R. Mackintosh, *The Christian Experience of Forgiveness*, Nisbet & Co 1927.

John Macquarrie, *In Search of Deity*, SCM Press 1984.

Warren McWilliams, *Divine Suffering in Contemporary Theology*, Scottish Journal of Theology, Vol. 33 (1980).

Emile Mersch, *The Whole Christ*, Denis Dobson 1936.

Thomas Merton, *The Sign of Jonas*, Hollis & Carter, 1953.

Thomas Merton, *The End of Man*, Burns and Oates 1962.

Thomas Merton, *No Man Is An Island*, Harcourt, Brace & Co 1955.

Thomas Merton, *The New Man*, Burns and Oates 1962.

Thomas Merton, *Elected Silence*, Burns and Oates 1961.

Elizabeth R. Moberly, *Suffering, Innocent and Guilty*, SPCK 1978.

R. C. Moberly, *Atonement and Personality* John Murray 1917.

Jürgen Moltmann, *The Crucified God*, SCM Press 1974.

Jürgen Moltmann, *Creation and Redemption*, Essay in *Creation Christ and Culture: Studies in Honour of T. F. Torrance*, Ed by Richard W. A. McKinney, T. & T. Clark 1976.

Jürgen Moltmann, *Experiences of God*, SCM Press 1980.

Jürgen Moltmann, *The Trinity and the Kingdom of God*, SCM Press 1981.

Jürgen Moltmann, *God in Creation*, SCM Press 1985.

A Monk of Marmion Abbey, *Becoming Christ*, Dimension Books: Denville New Jersey 1980.

Ed by Hugh Montefiore, *Man and Nature*, Collins 1975.

Sebastian Moore, *The Crucified Is No Stranger*, DLT 1977.

C. F. D. Moule, *The Origin of Christology*, CUP 1977.

*North – South: A Programme for Survival*, Report of the International Commission on International Development Issues, Pan Books 1980.

Wolfhart Pannenberg, *Future and Unity*, Essay in *Hope and the Future of Man*, Ed by Ewart H. Cousins, Garstone Press 1973.

A. R. Peacocke, *Creation and the World of Science*, Clarendon Press 1979.
'Pinions', *Wind on the Sand*, SPCK 1980.
Norman Pittenger, *After Death Life in God*, SCM Press 1980.
Norman Pittenger, *Picturing God*, SCM Press 1982.
John Polkinghorne, *One World*, SPCK 1986.
O. C. Quick, *The Gospel of the New World*, Nisbet and Co 1944.
Karl Rahner, *Foundations of Christian Faith*, DLT 1978.
Karl Rahner and Wilhelm Thüsing, *A New Christology*, Burns and Oates 1980.
Hastings Rashdall, *The Idea of Atonement in Christian Theology*, Macmillan & Co 1919.
Cyril C. Richardson, *The Eucharistic Sacrifice*, Anglican Theological Review, January 1950.
Ed. by Elizabeth C. Rohrbach, *Jung's Contribution to Our Time: The Collected Papers of Eleanor Bertine*, C. G. Putnam 1967.
Christopher Rowland, *Christian Origins*, SPCK 1985.
H. H. Rowley, *From Moses to Qumran*, Lutterworth Press 1964.
E. P. Sanders, *Jesus and Judaism*, SCM Press 1985.
Rupert Sheldrake, *The Rebirth of Nature*, Century 1990.
Ulrich Simon, *A Theology of Auschwitz*, Victor Gollancy 1967.
J. S. Smuts, *Holism and Evolution*, Victor Gollancz 1926.
R. W. Southern, *St Anselm and His Biographer*, CUP 1963.
Peter Spink, *Spiritual Man in a New Age* DLT 1980.
Alan M. Stibbs, *The Meaning of the Word 'Blood' in Scripture*, Tyndale Press 1948.
John Stott, *The Cross of Christ*, Inter-Varsity Press 1986.
J. J. Stoudt, *Sunrise to Eternity: A Study in Jacob Boehme's Life and Thought*, University of Philadelphia Press 1957.
Kenneth Surin, *Theology and the Problem of Evil*, Basil Blackwell 1986.
Stephen Sykes, *Christian Theology Today*, Mowbray 1983.
Stephen Sykes, *The Role of Story in the Christian Religion: An Hypothesis*, Journal of Literature and Theology, Vol. I. No. 1 (March 1987).
Ed. by Stephen Sykes, *Sacrifice and Redemption: Durham Essays in Theology*. CUP 1991.
John V. Taylor, *The Go-Between God*, SCM Press 1972.
Vincent Taylor, *Jesus and His Sacrifice*, Macmillan 1948.
L. S. Thornton, *The Common Life in the Boby of Christ*, Dacre Press 1963.
Paul Tillich, *The Shaking of The Foundations*, SCM Press 1957.
Paul Tillich, *Systematic Theology*, James Nisbet & Co 1960.
Leo Tolstoy, *War and Peace*, Trans. by Rosemary Edmonds, Penguin Books 1986.
T. F. Torrance, *The Trinitarian Faith*, T. & T. Clarke, 1988.
T. F. Torrance, *Christian Theology and Scientific Culture*, Christian Journals 1980.
A. Toynbee, *A Historian's Approach to Religion*.
G. Van Der Leeuw, *Religion in Essence and Manifestation*, Trans. by J. E. Turner, Peter Smith, Gloucester, Massachusetts 1967.

Laurens van der Post, *Jung and the Story of Our Time*, Hogarth Press 1976.

Laurens van der Post, *The Lost World of the Kalahari*, Penguin Books 1985.

W. H. Vanstone, *The Stature of Waiting*, DLT 1982.

G. B. Verity, *Life in Christ*, Longmans Green & Co. 1954.

René Voillaume, *The Living God*, DLT 1980.

Walter von Loewenich, *Luther's Theology of the Cross*, Trans. by Herbert J. A. Bouman, Christian Journals Belfast 1976.

Barbara Ward and René Dubos, *Only One Earth*, Andre Deutsch 1972.

J. Neville Ward, *Friday Afternoon*, Epworth Press 1982.

Keith Ward, *Holding Fast to God*, SPCK 1982.

Richard E. Weingart, *The Logic of Divine Love*, Clarendon Press 1970.

Herbert Weisinger, *Tragedy and the Paradox of the Fortunate Fall*, Routledge and Kegan Paul 1953.

B. F. Westcott, *The Victory of the Cross*, Macmillan & Co *1888*.

Elie Wiesel, *Night*, MacGibbon & Mee 1960.

Maurice Wiles, *God's Action in the World*, SCM Press 1986.

H. A. Williams, *Poverty, Chastity and Obedience*, Mitchell Beazley 1975.

H. A. Williams, *Becoming What I Am*, DLT 1977.

H. A. Williams, *The Joy of God*, Mitchell Beazley 1979.

H. A. Wiliams, *Tensions*, Mitchell Beazley 1979.

H. A. Williams, *True Resurrection*, Mitchell Beazley 1979.

Rowan Williams, *The Wound of Knowledge*, DLT 1979.

K. J. Woolcombe, *The Pain of God*, Scottish Journal of Theology, Vol. 20 (1967).

Peter Worsley, *Introducing Sociology*, Penguin Education 1976.

Frances Young, *Sacrifice and the Death of Christ*, SCM Press 1975.

Frances Young, *Can These Dry Bones Live?* SCM Press 1982.

J. Z. Young, *An Introduction to the Study of Man*, Clarendon Press 1971.

# INDEX OF BIBLICAL REFERENCES